TURN YOUR WORLD UPSIDE DOWN TO GET YOUR LIFE RIGHT SIDE UP

Reverse Thinking Based on *A Course in Miracles*

BOOK II: Health, Conflict, Fear and Happiness.

Reverend Diane C. Lund

#1 Amazon Bestselling Author

Interactive Book With Over 15 Introductory Videos

dianelundmiracles.com

Turn Your World Upside Down

DEEP GRATITUDE

I have deep and profound gratitude for Helen Schucman and Bill
Thetford, who brought *A Course in Miracles* into the world,
and to Gloria and Kenneth Wapnick, PhD,
founders of the Foundation for *A Course in Miracles*.

In addition, I want to thank Mary and Bruce Eagle,
my first teachers, as well as Gary Renard for his amazing book
The Disappearance of the Universe, which immensely helped me
and my study group with some core questions.

Thank you from the bottom of my heart
for your tireless work and enthusiasm for the course material.

WELCOME TO BOOK II:
Health, Conflict, Fear and Happiness.
Turn Your World UPSIDE DOWN to Get Your Life RIGHT SIDE UP
Reverse Thinking Based on *A Course in Miracles.*

When I first came across *A Course in Miracles*, I was not a big fan! I thought the course was too long, looked too much like the Bible and appeared to be loaded with Christian terminology. I had gone to church in my teenage years, but I had left it behind after my pastor had told me he did not have the answers to my many questions and suggested I go on a spiritual search to calm my questioning mind. I explored many different spiritual books and teachers, but a series of events pointed me back to *A Course in Miracles* and guided me to embrace its teachings. I attended a local study group in my area, and when my teachers moved on to another city, I started a study group in my own home.

Even though I was now leading this group, I did not think of myself as a teacher. Instead, I thought of myself as student who wanted and needed to explore the text with other students because quite frankly, I could not understand it. I wanted and needed other people's opinions and understandings to help me stay with the material. It was "a long and winding road," to quote the Beatles' song. I would gain some small understanding and then my ego would knock me back off my feet. My head knew the concept of what the text was presenting to me but working the principles into my everyday life was more difficult than I had expected. I have come to learn that this is a common experience with *A Course in Miracles*. You take in as much as you can, and then you need to do your own fieldwork. You get out there and you work at incorporating the ideas into your daily life. The material literally needs to fall from head into your heart. It is easy to say that we're all one, but to live from this deep understanding – to not judge and not criticize other people because you truly understand that the only person you hurt is yourself – takes time. You are undoing some very old patterns that are often firmly rooted in our culture, so be patient and gentle with yourself.

A Course in Miracles is not easy because it takes many of the concepts we take for granted in Western society and asks us to turn them upside down. In response, our personal egos fight this "turn of affairs."

The ego likes to be right; it is not interested in loving. It comes from fear, and it will fight for its beliefs and principles. It is frightened to let go of control and let God or the Holy Spirit take the helm. So, do not worry if this material seems strange and difficult, as it is strange and difficult for most Western cultures. However, I have found the rewards are deep and miraculous – just as the course promises.

In Book I, I shared my long personal history with *A Course in Miracles* and discussed fifteen key learnings from the text. Book II explores fifteen more of the ideas found in *A Course in Miracles* from the perspective of my own life and learning. As I said earlier, it is one thing to think you know something. It is another thing to put the ideas into practice, and still another for these ideas to become something you do without needing to think about it.

The stories in this book look at my experiences with *A Course in Miracles* upside-down thinking, including:
- How did I come to believe what I do?
- Where did I struggle with the material?
- How did I find a deeper, richer and more satisfying life?

Perhaps if you relate to my stories, you too will look beyond the surface to the eternal life that lives within each of us.

For those who did not read the first book and do not know much about *A Course in Miracles*, Book II reiterates what *A Course in Miracles* is. It then gives you my experience with the text and how you can look up the quotes. These sections may be repetitive if you are already familiar with the Course, so feel free to jump to the stories or to wherever you are intuitively drawn. There is no need to read this book from front to back; it is designed to let you read however the spirit moves you!

WATCH THE INTRODUCTORY VIDEOS BY SCANNING THE QR CODES

At the beginning of each chapter there is a short video on the main theme being discussed. All you have to do is scan the QR code on the chapter's first page and the video will play. If you do not already have a QR scanner on your phone, you can download one for free from your preferred app store.

All of the videos felt truly guided and full of spirit, and many were shot in just one take. It was amazing to see them unfold. There were no scripts and no plans. I simply trusted my inner guidance, and I was amazed to see the results. In many ways, creating these videos was a miracle for me, as I hope that watching them will be for you.

Many of the videos take place on the beautiful and charming property and home of Tracey and Andy Antliff in Bayac, France. Their place is called La Maison de la Libellule. You can find it online at the following link:

- www.facebook.com/lamaisondelalibellule/

TABLE OF CONTENTS

INTRODUCTION: *A COURSE IN MIRACLES*

PART ONE
HEALTH
Body Focus Versus Spirit Focus

Western Thinking: I need to improve.
Reverse Thinking: I am perfect.

Western Thinking: Sickness is in the body.
Reverse Thinking: Sickness is in the mind.

Western Thinking: I am a victim of the world I see.
Reverse Thinking: I am responsible for what I see.

Western Thinking: We rest when we are asleep.
Reverse Thinking: We rest when we are truly awake.

Western Thinking: Health is body wellness.
Reverse Thinking: Health is inner peace.

PART TWO
CONFLICT AND FEAR
How to Survive the Daily News

PART THREE
HAPPINESS
An Ideal Life Versus an Authentic Life

PART FOUR
LET'S GET PRACTICAL:
Putting Reverse Thinking Into Action

INTRODUCTION
A Course in Miracles

What does *A Course in Miracles* mean to me?
Watch this video and learn more.

Introduction: What *A Course In Miracles* Means To Me. *A Course in Miracles* is many things to me. The curriculum is to know thyself. Watch this video to learn how *A Course in Miracles* can change your life.

http://bit.ly/IntroBook1

A. WHAT IS *A COURSE IN MIRACLES*?

Many people may not have heard of *A Course in Miracles*, or, have heard the title but, are not sure what it is about. I think the book is well summarized in its own preface. Below is a brief summary of what it says.

SELF-STUDY SPIRITUAL THOUGHT SYSTEM

A Course in Miracles is a complete self-study spiritual thought system and a way through which some people will be able to find their own internal teacher. It is a three-step curriculum consisting of:
- *A Course in Miracles* text,
- a *Workbook for Students* containing 365 lessons, one for each day of the year, and
- a *Manual for Teachers*.

IT IS BUT ONE VERSION OF THE UNIVERSAL CURRICULUM

A Course in Miracles teaches that the way to universal love and peace – or remembering God – is by undoing guilt through forgiving others. The book focuses on healing relationships and making them holy (whole). It emphasizes that it is but one version of the universal curriculum, of which there are many. Consequently, even though the language of the course is that of traditional Christianity, it expresses a non-sectarian, non-denominational spirituality. *A Course in Miracles* is therefore a universal spiritual teaching, not a religion.

THE TEXT IS THEORETICAL

A Course in Miracles presents the theory of the course. . It presents two thought systems, the real and the unreal. The real world is under one law: the law of love, or God. There are no changes and no time. Truth is unalterable and eternal. On the other hand, the unreal world is the world of perception, which is based on time and change. It is the world of birth, death, and personal conflict.

Conflict arises because we all believe different things. To end the conflict, the course says we must first end the conflict in our minds between the two warring thought systems:
- The thought system of ego, which is based in sin, guilt and fear.
- The thought system of the Holy Spirit, which is based in love.

A Course in Miracles asks us to listen within to hear the Voice for God, which is the Holy Spirit.

The Holy Spirit was placed as a communication link between God and his creations when they decided to believe they had separated from Him. The Holy Spirit is the Voice for Love. The text explains the basis for fear and guilt and how they can be overcome through miracles, which are defined as maximal expressions of love, and so change perceptions (which are personal) into knowledge (which is eternal and non-personal).

THE WORKBOOK IS PRACTICAL

The Workbook for Students consists of 365 lessons – an exercise for each day of the year.

> *"Without the practical application the Workbook provides,*
> *the Text would remain largely a series of abstractions which would hardly suffice*
> *to bring about the thought reversal at which the course aims."*
>
> Preface: ix

This one-year training program begins the process of changing the student's mind and perceptions from fear-based thinking to love-based thinking. This year of lessons is not intended to bring one's learning to completion. As stated in the preface of the course:

> *"At the end, the reader is left in the hands of his or her own Internal Teacher,*
> *Who will direct all subsequent learning as He sees fit."*
>
> Preface: ix-x

THE MANUAL FOR TEACHERS

The Manual for Teachers is written in question-and-answer form and provides answers to some of the more common questions a student might ask. It also includes clarification on a number of terms the course uses, explaining them within the theoretical framework of the text as well as their practical application through the workbook.

WHO WROTE *A COURSE IN MIRACLES?*

A Course in Miracles was scribed by Dr. Helen Schucman, a clinical and research psychologist and tenured associate professor of medical psychology, through a process of inner dictation she identified as coming from Jesus. She was assisted by Dr. William Thetford, her department head and tenured professor of medical psychology at Columbia University's College of Physicians and Surgeons in New York City.

WHEN WAS *A COURSE IN MIRACLES* PUBLISHED?

A Course in Miracles was first published in 1975, the year Dr. Schucman assigned copyright of the course to the Foundation for Inner Peace (FIP). In 1996, FIP assigned the copyright and trademark to the Foundation for *A Course in Miracles* (FACIM).

There are currently millions of copies of the course in circulation worldwide. Translations in Afrikaans, Bulgarian, Chinese, Croatian, Danish, Dutch, Finnish, French, German, Hebrew, Italian, Norwegian,

Polish, Portuguese, Romanian, Russian, Slovene, Spanish, and Swedish are also available, with many other translations now in progress.

A COURSE IN MIRACLES SUMMED UP

The introductory section of *A Course in Miracles* text sums up the whole course in the following way:

"This is A Course in Miracles.
It is a required course.
Only the time you take it is voluntary.
Free will does not mean that you can establish the curriculum.
It means only that you can elect what you want to take at a given time.
The course does not aim at teaching the meaning of love,
for that is beyond what can be taught.
It does aim, however, at removing the blocks to the awareness of love's presence,
which is your natural inheritance.
The opposite of love is fear, but what is all-encompassing can have no opposite.

This Course can therefore be summed up very simply in this way:
Nothing real can be threatened.
Nothing unreal exists.
Herein lies the peace of God."

T, Introduction, 1-2

B. WHAT DOES *A COURSE IN MIRACLES* MEAN TO ME?

KNOW THYSELF.

A Course in Miracles is many things to me.

- It can provide a way to find your own internal teacher – the small, still voice within that speaks for God. In the course, this is referred to as the Holy Spirit.
- It is a course in mind training. It can train your mind to think from love in every situation.
- It is about unlearning wrong-minded thinking and moving into right-minded thinking or miracle-minded thinking.
- It is a return to love.
- It is a short and direct path to God or the love that is eternal.
- It is an individual spiritual study guide.

You do not need a study group to explore the course's teachings, but I have certainly found participating in and eventually leading *A Course in Miracles* reading and study groups to be extremely helpful. The concepts, while ultimately simple, usually bring up deep resistance from the ego part of the mind. Most of us have been taught a way to live, see, and be that is ultimately 180-degrees from what *A Course in Miracles* teaches. So, we need to change our thinking about what works and what doesn't.

Changing our thinking can be challenging, so having a support group to discuss the work has been comforting and necessary for my own process.

APPLICATION AND EXPERIENCE ARE KEY!

Finally, for me, the course emphasizes application rather than theory and experience rather than theology. You must experience the course concepts for yourself; no one can do this internal work for you. I love how the course puts it in the Introduction to the *Workbook for Students*.

> *"Remember only this; you need not believe the ideas,*
> *you need not accept them, and you need not even welcome them.*
> *Some of them you may actively resist.*
> *None of this will matter, or decrease their efficacy.*
> *But do not allow yourself to make exceptions in applying the ideas the workbook contains,*
> *and whatever your reactions to the ideas may be, use them.*
> *Nothing more than that is required."*
>
> W, Introduction, 9:1-4

Essentially, the course is not something you just read – it is something you must experience and ultimately prove to yourself. No one else can do it for you.

> *"I am responsible for what I see."*
>
> T, 21, II, 2:3

When you see that you can change your mind and your world, the real excitement begins. You are on the spiritual path to freedom. Personally, I have felt like a spiritual detective, hunting down the clues, following the signs that have led me to find more peace and happiness in my life. Ultimately, I believe *A Course in Miracles* is designed to lead everyone who follows it to their true authentic self and spiritual home.

C. HOW THIS BOOK IS ORGANIZED.

THE OPENING COUPLET

Western Thinking: this is the dominant thinking of the Western world, which is common but not universal. I say it is *Western thinking* because I believe *Eastern thinking* is often quite different.

Reverse Thinking: this is an opposite way of viewing the world from traditional Western thinking. It is the system of thought that is presented in the book *A Course in Miracles*.

MY PERSONAL EXPERIENCE

What follows the couplet is my personal experience with the reversal in thought, which shows how I came to believe many of them.

SUPPORTING QUOTES FROM *A COURSE IN MIRACLES*

Following my personal story is some reflection of the basic principle illustrated within it. This is followed by quotes from *A Course in Miracles* that reference where this principle is discussed in the book. If you feel intrigued, you can look up a quote and go deeper into this topic.

THERE ARE NO RULES; READ WHAT INTERESTS YOU IN ANY ORDER

There is no need to read this book from beginning to end. You can start in the middle, start at the end, or just open it and begin reading. There is no right way or wrong way, just your own **DIVINE INNER GUIDANCE (D.I.G.)** to point you to the sections that will be the most relevant for you.

D. HOW TO FIND QUOTES IN *A COURSE IN MIRACLES* (ACIM)

Published by the Foundation for Inner Peace
Combined Volume (Third Edition) copyrighted 2007 by the Foundation for *A Course in Miracles*
www.facim.org

Quotes from *A Course in Miracles* will be referenced in the following manner:

A Course in Miracles **TEXT**
T: Chapter, Section, Paragraph / Verse: Line

WORKBOOK FOR STUDENTS

W: Lesson Number, Section, Paragraph / Verse: Line

MANUAL FOR TEACHERS

M: Page Number, Section, Paragraph / Verse: Line

EXAMPLE: T, 9, V, 4:1-4

Text (T), Chapter Number (9), Subhead (V), Verse (4): Lines (1-4)

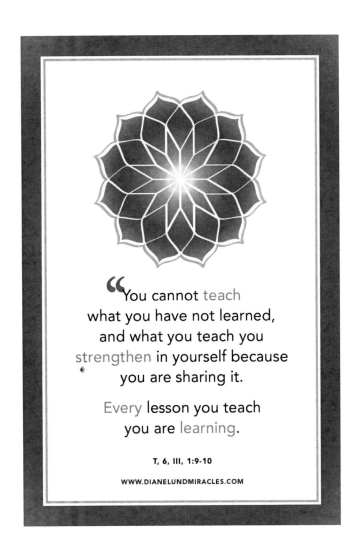

"You cannot teach
what you have not learned,
and what you teach you
strengthen in yourself because
you are sharing it.

Every lesson you teach
you are learning.

T, 6, III, 1:9-10

WWW.DIANELUNDMIRACLES.COM

PART ONE

HEALTH
Body Focus Versus
Spirit Focus

"Your upside-down perception
has been ruinous to your peace of mind.
You have seen yourself in a body and the truth outside you,
locked away from your awareness by the body's limitations.
Now we are going to try and see this differently."

W, L72, 8:3-5

# INTRODUCTION

HERE IS THE PROBLEM

There is so much attention and focus put on our bodies – especially for women. When I was growing up, I remember never feeling good enough. I started taking dance lessons at the age of five, and I was very aware that I needed to look good on stage if I wanted my dance teacher to be happy. By my teens, I started to diet because I believed my thighs were much too big. I had this belief validated in my senior high school year when I was doing a solo dance performance behind a screen. In the dance, I was supposed to be the living spirit of Mary Magdalene in the rock opera Jesus Christ Superstar. After a few rehearsals, I was told I would have to wear a flowing skirt over my leotard and tights because my thighs appeared too big on the screen.

Their perception proved what I already knew. I was not perfect. I was flawed. My body was to blame. Let me just say that I was not fat; I weighed about one hundred pounds at the time. However, you could not convince me of that reality at that time in my life.

We see what we want to see.

All this focus on our bodies can make us think, This is who I am: I am the person looking back at me from my mirror. Most of us do not look in the mirror and see our radiant spirit. Instead, we look in the mirror and see all our judgements.

- My feet are too big.
- My nose is too long.
- There is too much hair on my arms.
- My eyelashes are not long enough.

Then one day, you catch a glance of yourself in a window reflection and you ask yourself, "Who is that?" before you realize with deep surprise, "It is me!" Your body does not look like what you thought it did! This comes as a surprise, even though you know you certainly do not look the same at 5, 15, 25, 55, or 85 years old. Our body changes as we age, and the way we look changes along with it.

If I think I am just the image in the mirror, I could easily get depressed, anxious, critical, or sad. I might think, My youth is gone! In contrast, I found myself thinking, I look older, but I don't feel older. I think it is common to have both these thoughts.

The reason we do not feel older (even though we might look older) is because we are not our bodies. Our bodies will grow old and die here on the physical plane, but our spirit is eternal, whole, and pure – forever. We never change as spirit. This is truly our authentic being. We do not really age.

The body is just a costume of flesh and blood that our spirit inhabits in order to play here on the physical plane. In this life, I am playing the role and personality of Diane Christine Lund. However, that is not who I truly am. It is my belief that I am spirit: eternal love, ever extending and ever creating. I am the son/daughter of God.

FOCUSING ON OUR BODIES FOCUSES US ON JUDGING
When we focus on ourselves as bodies, we see ourselves as separate from others. Bodies seem to prove we are each a separate being. We create a lot of misery for ourselves with this type of thinking because we compare and contrast one body to another. We create hurtful thoughts such as:
- I am too big.
- My nose is too crooked.
- I am not as good-looking as her.
- I am not as muscular as him.
- I wish I had curly hair.
- I wish I had long hair.
- My eyes are too small.
- I am fat.

The list of complaints and judgements are long and varied; there are as many different thoughts as there are different people.

Bodies make our belief in separation seem very real. *A Course in Miracles* says that is what bodies are really for – they keep us believing in our separation from each other and from God.

> *"This is why you find what you seek.*
> *What you want in yourself you will make manifest,*
> *and you will accept it from the world because you put it there by wanting it."*
>
> T 12, IV, 7:4-5

FOCUS ON YOURSELF AS SPIRIT

When we change our focus from our bodies to our reality as spirit, we focus on our higher being and time can almost cease to exist.

We have all had this experience. You were dancing, you were playing, you were planting a garden, you were writing, or painting, or cooking, or even making love, and you lost all awareness of time. You looked up at the clock to see hours had passed when it felt like maybe just minutes had gone by. You were in the zone of creation.

It does not matter what you look like; what matters is how you feel about yourself. How do you identify yourself? Are you a body with limitations, or are you a free, eternal spirit with no limits? When we align with our true nature of our eternal love, the body can be a natural extension of this love. When we allow the care of the body to be directed by spirit, miraculous things can and do happen.

The following chapters explore how we can all learn to live from the inside out to have deeper, happier, and more fulfilling lives.

Chapter 1

PERFECTION: Do I Need to Improve?

Western Thinking
- I need to improve.

Reverse Thinking
- I am perfect.

**Chapter 1 – Perfection:
Do I Need to Improve?**
Everybody and everything seems to need improvement, according to our media. We are fed a steady diet of "helpful" tools and tips that serve to remind us we are not enough, just as we are. But, do we need to improve? Watch this video to find out.

bit.ly/perfectionimprove

I AM PERFECT:
MY PERSONAL EXPERIENCE WITH THIS REVERSE THOUGHT

Do we ever believe we are enough? Everything on the physical plane encourages us to improve – to keep growing, keep expanding, keep learning. At the bottom of it all is the terrible belief that we are not good enough, intellectual enough, loveable enough, beautiful enough, or talented enough (pick your poison).

We each have our own unique recipe for how we do not fit in or measure up. Often, we do not speak about these thoughts. The reason for this is simple: if we looked at our inner beliefs – if we brought it all up to the surface and discussed it – we might just discover we are right, and that would be horrifying. So instead we turn away, stuff it away, blame it away, curse it away, drink it away, or just simply run away all together. None of this helps. I know, because I grew up in an alcoholic family that did all of the above.

JUST BURY IT
No one was acknowledging the elephants in my family's living room. I begged my parents to talk to me about why we were all living this way. I pleaded with my mom, "Why can't we talk about the drinking, fighting, and yelling?"

The chaos in my home scared me. I wanted to be safe, but my mom just wanted me to bury it. That was my mom's favourite phrase: "Just bury it." But I knew I was not good at burying my problems. Often in the middle of the night, or at the most unusual times, my problems would just bubble back up right in my face like a monster that had been locked in the closet but was now free to wreak havoc on my world. How did that look?

- I would be overly emotional about something very insignificant.
- I would not be able to talk when someone asked me a question.
- I would cry for no good reason.
- I would be depressed when I judged I should be happy.

I wanted to understand why I felt the way I did. So, I pursued many personal growth programs and courses. One of my favourite teachers and mentors mixed drama with psychology, and this psychodramatic approach helped me uncover what I had locked or buried away for years.

ARMOURED AMAZON OR ETERNAL LITTLE GIRL?
The exact psychodrama course I took had a strange title: *Armoured Amazon or Eternal Little Girl?* The brochure stated that the course was going to explore the feminine archetypes in our life. I thought it sounded interesting, so I signed up.

On the first night of the course, we were asked to go to the costume room and dress up as our mother one week before her wedding. I choose a large red cloak, a white dress, and a little nurse's cap. I was dressed up as my mother, May, the way I thought she might have looked upon graduation from nursing school.

As we all emerged from the dressing room, we found our instructor standing behind a video camera, ready to tape our performances. One by one, we stepped into the spotlight and became our mothers.

When my turn came, I sat up on a big stool and settled my beautiful cape all around me. My instructor began by asking me some questions.

"Now May, it looks like you recently graduated. Tell me about that."

"Yes, I am thrilled to have gotten my nurse's cap and cape at my recent graduation from nursing school. It is all terribly exciting," I replied as my mother. "We worked very hard for the nuns that run our Catholic Nursing School. We got up early and were at work by 6:00 a.m., and often we did not quit until 6:00 p.m. The nuns were very strict, but I enjoyed my time there."

"That's wonderful, May. Congratulations. What is on the horizon for you next?" the instructor continued.

"Well, I am about to get married. Next week in fact," May announced with joy.

"That sounds wonderful! Can you tell me a little more about your upcoming marriage? Who are you marrying?"

"Well, my fiancé's name is Leo Lund, and he is a very talented architect. We met here in Victoria, but we are planning on moving to Vancouver after we marry. We think there are more opportunities there."

"What type of opportunities?"

"Leo is going to start his own architectural firm. He is a brilliant designer, and he wants to pursue his creative dreams. Then, perhaps we will start a family. We both want children."

"That certainly does sound like a bright future, May. Thank you for sharing." The instructor concluded the interview and turned off the recording.

After all the participants had gone in front of the camera, our instructor explained we now have on tape all of our mothers at one of the brightest moments in their lives. Then she announced that during the next class we would be turning the tables.

What does that mean? I wondered.

THE SHADOW SIDE OF THE FEMININE ARCHETYPE

When we came in the next day, we were asked to take a seat and review a variety of different mother archetypes that were written up on sheets of paper. Some examples include:

- The Ice Queen
- The Too-Good Mother
- The Wicked Witch
- The Armoured Amazon
- The Devouring Mother
- The Step-Mother
- The Eternal Little Girl
- The Fairy Godmother

There were twelve distinct feminine archetypes, all of which had both good and not-so-good qualities.

The instructor explained, "Yesterday was all about your mothers at their best. Now, we will look at their shadow sides." We were asked to pick the archetype we thought our mothers acted out when they were at their worst.

I knew immediately which archetype I would dress up as – my mother was clearly the wicked witch when she was at her worst. So, I got to work. This time, I choose an all-black outfit. I slicked back my hair and tied it up into a tight bun. Finally, I powdered my face so I looked pasty white and tired.

When the video camera turned on, I was ready for my cameo. I put myself back up on the tall stool, and then my instructor inquired, "May, you are looking a little worn and tired. What's wrong?"

"What's wrong? Do you have to ask? The house is a mess. There are dishes to do, a floor to wash, a stew to make, and a garden to plant. I have to get busy or I will never get it all done," I complained bitterly.

"Do you have to do all that work by yourself, May? Isn't there someone who can help?"

"Heavens, no. I cannot possibly do all that work myself – that's why I have three daughters! They need to work for their room and board. There will be no lazy bones lying about here! I need them all to get to work now."

"I see. Is that your daughter over there? She is sitting down reading a book. What do you want to tell her to do?" the instructor asked.

"Diane, stop reading that book and get over here right now and help me cut up these vegetables for the stew. And do not cut them that way. That is the wrong way. Give me that knife. Let me show you once again how it is done. Like this, not like that. Now get to work," the wicked witch insisted.

"Does your daughter often get it wrong, May? I notice she was not cutting the vegetables the right way."

"These girls just do not know how to do things properly. I always have to get on their backs and watch their every move. I just cannot trust them. I have to keep on them!"

"That must be hard on you. You do look tired."

"I am tired. I am sick and tired of all there is to do around here. It is very hard on me to have to do my work and then watch over them too. I need them to work faster. Work harder. There is just a never-ending list of things that must get done around here. I can't have them watching television or reading books all the time."

"Yes, I can see that. What do you want to tell your daughters, May?"

"Well, they simply are not working hard enough. They must work harder or we will never get ahead."

"Working harder – is that the secret, May?"

"Absolutely. Those daughters of mine must work harder. That's what I had to do in nursing school. I was up early every morning, scrubbing floors, getting bedpans, walking the halls for hours. No one helped me. Those lazy bones have it easy around here."

There it was, coming directly out of my mouth:
- the voice I heard in my head,
- the voice that told me what to do,
- the voice that said work harder.

Work harder! it yelled. *Work harder!*

With horror, I realized the voice in my head was the wicked witch, and unfortunately it was alive and well!

Suddenly, it started to dawn on me why I put in such ridiculously long days at the office. The voice in my head was clearly telling me I needed to work harder and do more. It was the very first time I realized my mother's voice was running the show! And that voice was harsh and stern. It did not allow room for play and laughter. It wanted compliance and hard work and nothing short of perfection. It was, without a doubt, a no-nonsense, no-feeling, wicked old witch.

Once the camera turned off and we all changed out of our costumes, we came back together to examine and explore what we had learned.

For me, the learning was clear and profound. The voice in my head that told me to work harder was my mother's voice. Even though she was not in the room, I was carrying her around in my mind. I was listening to her judgments, and I was still trying to make things perfect in my mom's eyes.

"And how did it make you feel to play your mother this time?" my instructor asked.

"It was uncomfortable and difficult. I did not like what I was saying," I replied.

"Do you think your mother was uncomfortable and unhappy when she was yelling at you like that?" my instructor asked.

"Yes. When I was playing the wicked witch, I could feel her deep unhappiness," I said as I hung my head.

"Do you think from now on, you could feel compassion for your mother and for yourself whenever you hear those words, 'work harder?' Clearly your mother was in pain. Can you open your heart to her, and to yourself?"

Playing the shadow part of my mother, I had truly felt her depression and desperation. She was not happy. My heart began to open to the plight of my mom, and to her pain. I could feel the unhappiness that drove her to push us, and suddenly I felt compassion and love for my mom.

"Yes," I said, "I can feel compassion for my mother in her situation. She had a drunken husband, she did not drive, and she felt trapped. She wanted out, and she did not know how to escape. She was a prisoner of her own making."

"And what about you, Diane. Isn't it time for you to be free too? You no longer need to be driven by your mother's critical voice. When you hear yourself telling yourself to work harder, perhaps you can stop and feel compassion for yourself, and then choose another way of responding besides overworking."

The instructor's words made perfect sense. I did not need to improve. I did not need to work harder. There was nothing wrong with me. There was just a voice in my head – a voice from the past that I could let go of, once and for all.

I was never going to be perfect enough for my mother. I was never going to be able to work hard enough or long enough. I would never do enough or achieve enough to satisfy the wicked witch within. It was time to put it all down:

- all the complaints about myself, and
- all the complaints about my mother.

And as I lay the past at my feet and looked into my heart, I felt the love from within radiate outwards. I felt peace. I felt calm. I felt perfectly me, without doing anything at all.

“Miracles are
teaching devices
for demonstrating
it is as blessed to give
as to receive.

T, 1, 16:1

WWW.DIANELUNDMIRACLES.COM

WHAT DOES *A COURSE IN MIRACLES* SAY ABOUT PERFECTION?

When I was younger, I felt a drive to be perfect: to get perfect grades, to be the perfect weight, to be the perfect girlfriend. However, what I learned as I stepped into leadership roles surprised me: no one really wants perfect, they want real.

When we see someone who is perfect (in our opinion), we often do not like them. We judge them. We criticize them. We try to bring them down a notch or two, because we do not like comparing ourselves to someone we judge as being better than us.

This is an ego game, and it never makes us feel any better. It brings up feelings of guilt, shame, unworthiness, and sadness. It's a no-win scenario.

In our dualistic physical world, nothing is perfect because everything is changing. A beautiful blooming flower never remains the same; it is in the process of changing its physical appearance, just as we are. Our change is slower than that of the flower, but when we compare ourselves to photographs of us from ten or twenty years ago, we can see the truth in this matter. Our spirit, however, does not change – it is eternal and perfect. We are the perfection we seek.

WITHIN YOU IS EVERYTHING THAT IS PERFECT
"Deep within you is everything that is perfect, ready to radiate through you and out into the world."
W, L41, 3:1

THE PERFECT COMFORT THAT COMES FROM PERFECT REST
"The children of God are entitled to the perfect comfort that comes from perfect rest. Until they achieve this, they waste themselves and their true creative powers on useless attempts to make themselves more comfortable by inappropriate means."
T, 2, III, 5:1-2

HE CREATED THEM PERFECT
"The atonement is the only gift that is worthy of being offered at the altar of God, because of the value of the altar itself. It was created perfect and is entirely worthy of receiving perfection. God and His creations are completely dependent on Each Other. He depends on them because He created them perfect."
T, 2, III, 5:5-7

THERE MUST BE A BETTER WAY

"Tolerance for pain may be high, but it is not without limit. Eventually everyone begins to recognize, however dimly, that there must be a better way. As this recognition becomes more firmly established, it becomes a turning point. This ultimately reawakens spiritual vision, simultaneously weakening the investment in physical sight. The alternating investment in the two levels of perception is usually experienced as conflict, which can become very acute. But the outcome is as certain as God."

T, 2, III, 3:5-10

THE END OF ILLUSION

"Every miracle is but the end of an illusion."

T, 19, IV, A, 6:8

Chapter 2

SICKNESS:
Where Is It Located?

Western Thinking
- Sickness is in the body.

Reverse Thinking
- Sickness is in the mind.

Chapter 2 – Sickness: Where Is It Located?
Most of us consider sickness as being located in the body. *A Course in Miracles* teaches us that sickness is actually the body responding to what the mind is thinking and feeling. Watch the video to discover what is required if we want to attain true wellness.

bit.ly/sicknesswhere

SICKNESS IS IN THE MIND:
MY PERSONAL EXPERIENCE WITH THIS REVERSE THOUGHT.

According to many people, your health can be affected by time, weather, fatigue, food, drink, germs, herbs, medicine, ethnic origin, weight, hormones, whatever we make up, and these laws change with the ages. We believe we are victim to the world around us – or rather, we believe these laws affect us. We give them power, and by doing so we replace the power of God within us with the power of idols outside of ourselves. In contrast, *A Course in Miracles* says sickness is not an accident or something that just came upon us, but rather the result of what we believe.

- We believe we can be sick.
- We believe we can be less than perfect.
- We believe we can be less than everything.

Getting sick proves that this line of thought is correct. See, I am not perfect, I am not whole, because I am ill. Of course, these thoughts and beliefs are most often unconscious, buried deep within us. Like a giant iceberg, most of it lies below the surface.

Sickness, in essence, preserves the ego's thought system. This next story explains how I turned a sickness experience into a holy experience.

SICKNESS IN KAUAI

My husband and I were on holiday in Kauai, and we had brought my mother along. She had been suffering from polymyalgia – an inflammatory disorder that causes chronic pain and stiffness in the muscles – ever since my dad's death a couple of years before, as well as arthritis in her spine. So, we rented her a wheelchair for travel.

Our plane arrived late to the Honolulu airport, so we had to run to the other terminal to get a local flight to the island of Kauai. My mom got quite the bumpy ride as we pushed her in her wheelchair across different floors, cement sidewalks, and door jams. It was jarring for her body. All the bumpy movement in the wheelchair ride irritated her back, and from that moment on she had troubles.

A week later, her foot was very swollen and her leg was in terrible pain. So, we decided to phone her medical insurance and get her some treatment. We first went to the Koala walk-in medical clinic, but they sent us to Wilcox Memorial Hospital in Lihue.

At the same time, my husband needed care for an infected ear. He had been listening to my mother complain this whole time, and I knew he wanted her to stop. In my belief, he manifested an ear infection so he could not hear my mom. Between the two of them, there was a lot of pain and a distinctive lack of hearing.

The clinic sent us to the emergency room for tests. There we met a very handsome young doctor who had mom undergo an ultrasound and back x-rays. The final diagnosis was sciatica, so he prescribed pain medication. Then, my husband got treated.

Eight hours after we arrived at the hospital we finally made our way to Walmart to get the prescriptions filled. It was a tiring and exhausting day, but here is the amazing part. Everyone had reason to be in pain. My mom was miserable, suffering with sciatica. My husband had an ear infection and could not hear. My beloved dog had also died just a few days before. But amazingly, as we sat there waiting for our prescriptions, I was not experiencing any discomfort at all. In fact, I was having this beautiful experience. Instead of seeing the two of them as sick, I was seeing them as beautiful lights. All I saw was their joy and their love.

My mother would cry, "I feel awful. I am hurting." I would say, "I totally understand that you are hurting, Mom, but I am seeing you as the perfect light and love of God. I can't lie. When I look at you, I do not see sickness, I see beauty. I see your light."

She responded by swearing at me. "I am feeling miserable. I am not the light and love of God."

To which I said, "But that is how I see you Mom."

She grumbled unhappily.

These conversations between us continued, on and on, for the entire month-long trip. I was not pretending with my mother or trying to put on airs – I was truly in this amazing space where I saw her and everyone else as their true spiritual selves. They emanated light. I felt joyous even while I was surrounded by pain and suffering. It was an amazing time for me, and I will always look back on the experience fondly.

When we returned home, my two sisters were shocked. "What did you do to Mom?" they asked.

"Why?" I inquired.

"Well, she seems happy, and she keeps telling us she is the light and love of God."
Now it was my turn to be shocked. I had not thought my mother responded well to my perception of her

while we were away, but I guess I was wrong. Some of what I had said to her had gotten into her being. Something had shifted. She told my sister what I had told her: that she was the light and love of God.

Wow! I thought. She had a shift in perception from thinking from fear to thinking from love. This is the definition of a miracle from *A Course in Miracles*.

Was my mother in pain?
I am sure she was.

Was she the light and love of God?
I am sure she is.

WE PERCEIVE WHAT WE WANT TO PERCEIVE

Where we choose to put our perception is where we live and what we experience. We are the eternal light and love of God, even when our bodies feel pain. The pain and sickness we experience are trying to convince us we are not eternal beings – that we are bodies that die. If we choose to focus only on this physical level and these thoughts of death, we reinforce what we fear. We make it real for ourselves.

During my trip to Kauai, I chose to focus on my mother's spiritual reality while she chose to focus on her body reality. She did not like my perception when we were in Kauai, yet once she got home, she shifted her focus from her body to her spirit. She did not instantly become better upon making that change, but she did feel better and seemed happier than she had been in a very long time.

That is the goal of *A Course in Miracles*: to help you live a happier life no matter what is going on in your physical world.

This does not mean that you ignore your body. In fact, your body gives you signals as to whether you are in alignment with love or with fear. When you listen to these feelings, you can take the physical medicine you need, but you can also pay attention to what these signals tell you.

Start by asking yourself, what thoughts are fear-based? What is giving you a pain in the neck? Do you think your boss is a pain in the neck? Perhaps if you shifted your perception of your boss while also going to the chiropractor or massage therapist you might find even greater relief.

The course says it is foolish to ignore the body – after all, you are here on the dualistic physical plane. However, when you understand that you are more than just your body, then you can clearly decide where you want your focus and beliefs to live.

"When you want only love you will see nothing else."
T, 12, VII, 8:1

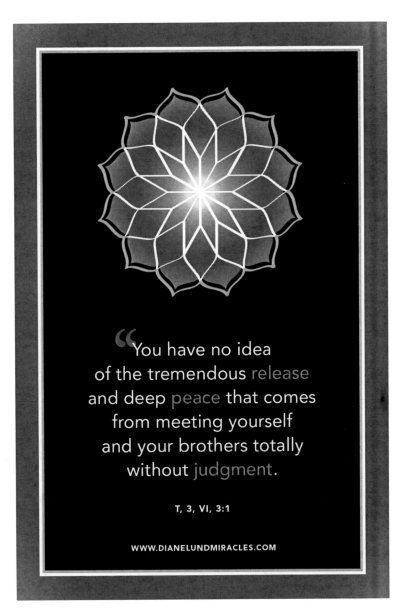

"You have no idea
of the tremendous release
and deep peace that comes
from meeting yourself
and your brothers totally
without judgment.

T, 3, VI, 3:1

WWW.DIANELUNDMIRACLES.COM

WHAT DOES *A COURSE IN MIRACLES* SAY ABOUT SICKNESS?

Sickness and health are sacred cows to many, many people. When I talk about this subject in my study groups, I can feel the tension in the room. Everybody has a long-held belief that they want to cling to, so few people are excited to change their minds. Most of us will cling to one or more of the many possible models for wellbeing:

- A medical model
- A chiropractic model
- A Chinese medicine model
- An alternative health model
- A family recipe model
- A nutrition model

These models help us make sense of the pain and sickness we may or may not be experiencing. They give us a physical way to move forward through our worlds, and that does serve a purpose. However, I am sure you will agree that most of these models shift and change with the times. For example, doctors one hundred years ago certainly believed and practiced different forms of healing than what we do today. The same will be true one hundred years from now.

A Course in Miracles looks at health as inner peace. It says sickness proves to us that we are mortal, not eternal, and that sick thoughts are rooted in fear-based thinking or wrong-minded thoughts. This thinking is mostly unconscious – we picked it up from our culture, our religions, our community, our health care professionals, our family, and many, many other sources.

The course asks you to remember that you are more than a body. You are part of the "one son," the eternal spirit that is eternal light and love. Acknowledging and giving thanks for this inner knowledge aligns you with love. God, or the Father, or the Source, is light, and that light is love. It is in all things.

When we are sick, we do not need to blame ourselves or anyone else; to do so would be counterintuitive because blame is rooted in fear. Instead, we simply need to shift our perspective from being body-focused to being focused on our true reality, our one whole (holy) spirit that is eternal love. From this perspective, we align with the truth within ourselves, and we start to heal the feeling that we are separate. This belief in separation, sickness, and death is what needs the real healing.

The good news is we can choose to change our perceptions. This does not mean we will be instantly healed, but it will open the way for miracles to appear in your life.

SICKNESS IS A DEFENSE AGAINST THE TRUTH

"I have forgotten what I really am, for I mistook my body for myself. Sickness is a defense against the truth. But I am not a body. And my mind cannot attack. So, I cannot be sick."

W, L136, 20:3-6

HEALTH IS INNER PEACE

"Illness is some form of external searching. Health is inner peace. It enables you to remain unshaken by lack of love from without and capable, through your acceptance of miracles, of correcting the conditions proceeding from lack of love in others."

T, 2, I, 5:9-11

HEALTH RELINQUISHES ALL ATTEMPTS TO USE THE BODY LOVELESSLY

"Health is the result of relinquishing all attempts to use the body lovelessly. Health is the beginning of the proper perspective on life under the guidance of the one Teacher who knows what life is, being the Voice for Life Itself."

T, 8, VIII, 9:9-10

SICKNESS IS NOT AN ACCIDENT

"Sickness is not an accident. Like all defences, it is an insane device for self-deception. And like all the rest, its purpose is to hide reality, attack it, change it, render it inept, distort it, twist it, or reduce it to a little pile of unassembled parts. The aim of all defences is to keep the truth from being whole. The parts are seen as if each one were whole within itself."

W, L136, 2:1-5

SICKNESS IS A DECISION

"Sickness is a decision. It is not a thing that happens to you, quite unsought, which makes you weak and brings you suffering. It is a choice you make, a plan you lay, when for an instant truth arises in your deluded mind, and all your world appears to totter and prepares to fall. Now are you sick, that truth may go away and threaten our establishments no more."

W, L136, 7:1-4

HOW DOES SICKNESS SHIELD YOU FROM THE TRUTH?

"Because it proves the body is not separate from you, and so you must be separate from the truth. You suffer pain because the body does, and in this pain are you made one with it. Thus is your 'true' identity preserved, and the strange, haunting thought that you might be something beyond this little pile of dust silenced and stilled."

W, L136, 8:1-4

SICKNESS OR NOT-RIGHT-MINDEDNESS

"Sickness or 'not-right-mindedness' is the result of level confusion, because it always entails the belief that what is amiss on one level can adversely affect another. We have referred to miracles as the means of correcting level confusion, for all mistakes must be corrected at the level on which they occur. Only the mind is capable of error. The body can act wrongly only when it is responding to misthought. The body cannot create, and the belief that it can, a fundamental error, produces all physical symptoms. Physical illness represents a belief in magic."

T, 2, IV, 2:2-7

SICKNESS COMES FROM SEPARATION

"All sickness comes from separation. When separation is denied, it goes. For it is gone as soon as the idea that brought it has been healed and been replaced by sanity. Sickness and sin are seen as consequence and cause, in a relationship kept hidden from awareness that it may be carefully preserved from reason's light."

T, 26, VII, 2:1

HEALING IS OF GOD

"Healing is of God in the end."

ST, 1, VII, 5:9

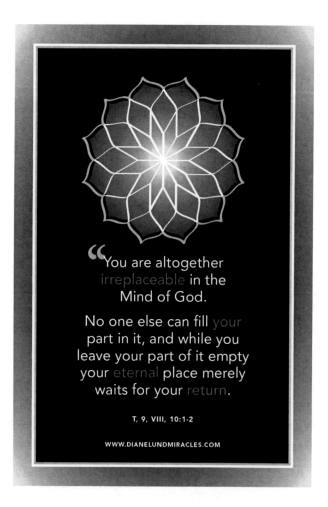

"You are altogether irreplaceable in the Mind of God.

No one else can fill your part in it, and while you leave your part of it empty your eternal place merely waits for your return.

T, 9, VIII, 10:1-2

WWW.DIANELUNDMIRACLES.COM

Chapter 3

RESPONSIBILITY:
Am I a Victim?

Western Thinking
- I am a victim of the world I see.

Reverse Thinking
- I am responsible for what I see.

Chapter 3 -
Responsibility: Am I a Victim?
The news is full of victim stories. Most of us have felt like a victim at one time or another. We can feel like a victim of the world we see, or we can take responsibility for the way we see the world. Watch this video to find out how *A Course in Miracles* helped me lose that "victim mentality."

bit.ly/responsevictim

I AM RESPONSIBLE FOR WHAT I SEE:
MY PERSONAL EXPERIENCE WITH THIS REVERSE THOUGHT

Everyone has no doubt felt like the victim of something at one time or another. To feel like a victim is to believe you are less, or are getting less, than you deserve. The course never aligns with this type of thinking. Instead, the course's perspective is that you are spirit, whole and complete; therefore, concepts of "less than" are illusions and not real. It is only misperceptions of your true being that create this idea of victims and victimhood.

Have you ever been in a situation where you thought someone said something to hurt you, but upon discussion, you learned they never intended to hurt you with their comment? Suddenly, you could change what you heard or saw in those words. This is literally the process of responsibility: seeing a situation one way and then having the strength of mind to see it from a new angle.

Rather than hurting ourselves through the actions of others, we can see what they do as a "call for love." We can understand that they are hurting, and that they project this hurt out onto the world (and us) in order to feel better. The course says this is the call for love. When we choose to look at things differently, we take responsibility for what we see. We can then turn the situation around from one that hurts us to one based in love and compassion. I believe this is the ultimate work in all our lives. Here's a story from my life that highlights this principle of being responsible.

A CALL FOR LOVE

After working in advertising and communications for a decade, I decided that I wanted more meaningful work. So, I went to The Haven Institute to take personal growth courses and ultimately do a Diploma in Counselling. During a month-long program entitled Phase One: Self, I learned my boyfriend was involved in many affairs. It was extremely painful. However, my instructors urged me not to run away from the pain, but instead to explore what was truly going on in my internal life by asking myself questions like:

- What had led me to this point?
- Did I want out of my misery?

Of course, the answer to the last question was "yes!" So, when I was challenged to come back and do another month-long program entitled Phase Two: Self and Others, I answered the call to explore my personal issues more deeply.

There was just one weekend between the end of Phase One and the beginning of Phase Two, and the weather was beginning to get colder. I needed to get home, pack warmer clothes, and let the people in my life know I would not be returning home for yet another month.

I went home on a Friday night and called my mom Saturday morning to inform her what was going on. She said she would like to see me before my departure on Sunday as she had some important information for me.

I spent the rest of the day washing clothes and packing for the upcoming month. I talked to friends on the phone and updated everyone on what I was setting out to do. I explained what I had learned in Phase One about my relationship and that I was in deep pain over the discovery. I needed help, and The Haven was offering it. I needed to go back.

The next morning, my mother came over to my apartment for breakfast. I told her about Phase One and my different revelations and discoveries – both the agony and the ecstasy. My mom was intrigued and listened closely.

Then she said, "I wanted to come over and say goodbye".

I said that was nice, but a month would fly by.

"No," she explained, "I am saying 'goodbye' for good."

"What do you mean?"

"I have decided to take my own life."

"What?" I asked, unable to believe what I had just heard. "How are you going to do that?"

"I am going to jump from a bridge."

"Why would you ever DO should a thing?"

"Well, I have tried and tried with your Dad, and his drinking and fighting are all just too much. I am too tired, and I just don't want to live anymore," she sighed.

Hmm… I thought. The instructors at The Haven had talked a fair bit about how people can believe that ending their life is a way out – that it may appear to be a solution on this physical level – when of course it is not.

So, after a long silence and some careful thought, I said, "I can see how you might think this way, Mom. I have been with you every step of the way, and I know how hard you have tried and how hard it has been. I can see that ending your life could appear to be a way out."

"Yes," she said, "I have made up my mind and wanted you to know."

Hmm… I thought again. The wheels were rapidly turning in my brain. This was totally unexpected, and I was surprised that I could remain so calm. However, my past month at The Haven had oddly prepared me for this terrible moment. I knew I could see myself as a victim of a terrible decision, or I could see the opportunity that lay in this terrible decision. I knew I needed to stay calm and not overreact.

"When are you planning this?" I asked quietly.

"This week sometime," she answered, as if she was talking about going downtown to a department store for a shoe sale.

"Okay," I said. "Well, I truly appreciate you telling me your decision. But what if there was another option? Think about this. If you have lived all these years and your final decision is to kill yourself, I can understand it. But what if there was another way? What if you took a month and came to The Haven with me? They have a totally different way of looking at the world, and maybe you will come to a different conclusion. If not, in a month, you can still jump off the bridge. It will still be there. I think you owe it to yourself, Mom, to try a path you have never taken before."

"Well, I can't do that!" she exclaimed.

"Why not?"

"Because I have guests staying at our house. What will they think if I just leave them high and dry?"

"Mom," I explained calmly, "you are planning to jump off a bridge – that's totally leaving them high and dry. If you can do that, surely you can leave them and put off your own death for a month. Try a new way. The Haven has totally shifted things for me, and I know it can do the same for you. I am not going to take no for an answer. I am going to get packed, and we are going to drive to your place. I will wait in the car while you run into the house and pack a bag. You can tell your guests that I need you and that you need to go to The Haven to help me – your daughter!"

After some thought, she said, "Okay, I'll go!"

I seized the moment. I was determined to see this differently. This was not a moment for me to crumble into victimhood with cries of Why me? This was my time to be strong: to hear my mother's plan, not as reason for me to dissolve into tears, but as her lonely and desperate cry for love. God was opening a door for my mother, and I needed to help her walk through it.

Determined, I rose from the kitchen table and quickly finished my packing. Then, we went in separate cars to my parent's home. I kept true to my word and waited in the car for my mom. She was true to her word and quickly packed. She told her houseguests there was an emergency she needed to immediately attend to with her daughter, and she headed out to meet me in my car.

It was done. My mom was now with me on the road less travelled. We were both heading to The Haven to literally save our lives!

When I look back at that awful day, I realize that I chose to take what could have potentially been a family disaster and turned it around in my mind to the ultimate family opportunity. We both needed healing, and doing it together was something I will always remain grateful for – it was an opportunity of a lifetime.

Together, we went to The Haven. Together, we both learned how to not be a victim, and to become responsible for our lives.

•

WHAT DOES *A COURSE IN MIRACLES* SAY ABOUT RESPONSIBILITY?

I have run study groups for *A Course in Miracles* out of my home for decades, and we always start by reading one of my favourite passages:

"I am responsible for what I see.
I choose the feelings I experience,
and I decide upon the goal I would achieve.
And everything that seems to happen to me
I ask for, and receive as I have asked.
Deceive yourself no longer that you are helpless
in the face of what is done to you.
Acknowledge but that you have been mistaken,
all effects of your mistakes will disappear."

T, 21, II, 2:3-7

At the end of the reading, I often ask a question: "What if we really took the words 'I am responsible for what I see' to heart?"

The quote does not say I am responsible for what is going on around me. It says, "I am responsible for what I see."

Responsibility is the key to unlocking your mind. If you take responsibility for "what you see," you begin to understand that you made up what you see.

In the previous story from my life, I could have seen my mom's confession as a reason to fall apart or to become a victim. Instead I turned that exact moment into an opportunity for healing.

Another important part of this reading is the quote, "I choose the feelings I experience, and I decide upon the goal I would achieve. And everything that seems to happen to me I ask for and receive as I have asked." Yes, I decide – not the government, or my parents, or my relatives.

Wow, that is a big, big claim. Surely, I am NOT responsible for everything. But the Course is unwavering in its position: yes, EVERYTHING.

Does that mean I cannot pick and choose what I'd like to be responsible for? Generally, people like to pick and choose. Do I pick this side or that side? Do I accept this idea or reject it? *A Course in Miracles* says we are always picking from one thought system or another. We can think from love or think from fear, And whichever one we pick is how we will see the world.

In addition, *A Course in Miracles* says there are no neutral thoughts. By claiming our responsibility and not giving it away to others, we take back control of our lives and ultimately our happiness.

I HAVE NO NEUTRAL THOUGHTS
"The idea for today is a beginning step in dispelling the belief that your thoughts have no effect. Everything you see is the result of your thoughts. There is no exception to this face. Thoughts are not big or little; powerful or weak."
W, L16, 1:1-4

I HAVE INVENTED THE WORLD I SEE
"You are not the victim of the world you see because you invented it. You can give it up as easily as you made it up. You will see it or not see it, as you wish. While you want it you will see it; when you no longer want it, it will not be there for you to see."
W, L32, 1:2-5

EVERY THOUGHT YOU HAVE CONTRIBUTES TO TRUTH OR ILLUSION
"There is no more self-contradictory concept than that of 'idle thought.' What give rise to the perception of a whole world can hardly be called idle. Every thought you have contributes to truth or to illusion; either it extends the truth or it multiplies illusions."
W, L16, 2:1-3

WE WILL REVERSE THE WAY YOU SEE
"We will reverse the way you see by not allowing sight to stop before it sees. We will not wait before the shield of hate, but lay it down and gently lift our eyes in silence to behold the son of God."
W, L78, 2:2-3

WHAT YOU DO COMES FROM WHAT YOU THINK
"You may believe that you are responsible for what you do, but not for what you think. The truth is that you are responsible for what you think, because it is only at this level that you can exercise choice. What you do comes from what you think."
Marianne Williamson, A Return to Love: Reflections on the Principles of *"A Course in Miracles"*

Chapter 4

REST: Where Do I Find Rest?

Western Thinking
- We rest when we are asleep.

Reverse Thinking
- We rest when we are truly awake.

Chapter 4 – Rest: Where Do I Find Rest?
How can we attain true, rejuvenating rest? Watch this video to discover how *A Course in Miracles* defines rest. Spoiler alert: it's not attained from a deep sleep, but from a deep spiritual awakening.

bit.ly/restwhere

WE REST WHEN WE ARE TRULY AWAKE:
MY PERSONAL EXPERIENCE WITH THIS REVERSE THOUGHT

I love the big questions in life. One of the things I have often heard people say in my spiritual search is that most of us are asleep here on planet earth. In fact, *A Course in Miracles* raises the point that the Bible says that Adam fell asleep, but nowhere does it say he awoke. In addition, *A Course in Miracles* refers to people as sleeping here on the physical plane. However, the course is NOT talking about what can be seen with our physical eyes.

What follows are a couple of stories about how spirit has moved me to awaken and find where true rest resides.

WAKE UP! WAKE UP!

When I was in my late twenties, I had a dream where I heard a voice yelling at me, Wake up! Wake up!

I awoke and instantly knew what it meant: I was asleep to myself, and it was time I started to wake up to who I truly was inside. The question then was, how exactly do I wake up? When I physically look around, people certainly look awake to me. They don't look like they are sleep walking or about to nod off. So, what exactly does that mean? Years later, while studying *A Course in Miracles*, I had an ah-ha moment (don't you just love those?) about these questions.

Out of the blue, it suddenly dawned on me that we are all asleep in the dream of the world. We are taught certain ideas, rules, and principles by our culture, family, religions, schools, friends, books, and media that literally put our minds to sleep. We don't see the world anew; rather, we see the world as we are taught to see it.

Some people call this process growing up.

As we live in our physical, dualistic world, we encounter a world of opposites. We learn the difference between things: right and wrong, cold and hot, winter and summer, all depending, of course, on where we live and what our elders teach us. Before long, most of us fall asleep to our inner selves. We don't question things anymore. We believe the status quo. We are slowly hypnotized into believing what everyone around us believes because we want to belong. We desire acceptance and love, and we do not want to be separated from everyone else. So, we buy into what everyone else says we should believe. And if we step outside this "box of thought," we can appear to others as foolish and even crazy.

WE SLEEP TOGETHER

What I finally understood was simple: just as I had heard many spiritual teachers say, the world is the dream, and we are dreaming it together. This dream is a nightmare if you believe the ego's perspective of pain and suffering. However, if you see beyond the physical illusionary world and behold the truth within all of us – that we are eternal, endless love, and that everyone and everything is made from this essence – then the dream can be a happy one. Here's how I turned my dream into a happy one and how I learned to find true rest.

REST IN ME

I had been studying *A Course in Miracles* for many, many years by holding groups in my home, but I was not totally committed. I was still at the spiritual smorgasbord. I was reading all types of books on the subject, such as *The Autobiography of a Yogi* by Paramahansa Yogananda.

I loved eastern mysticism – my home is covered in statues of many different spiritual icons, from Buddha to Kuan Yin. I was enjoying an eclectic spiritual mix, and I did not think *A Course in Miracles* would be my one path.

Until one day, when the unthinkable happened.

In my meditation, Jesus appeared to me in my mind's eye like a shining light. Inwardly, I heard the words, **Rest in me.** Then I saw myself falling through the air and being caught in the hands of Jesus like a small doll.

I came out of the meditation shocked. Jesus? I thought I had left conventional religion years ago. Even though *A Course in Miracles* identifies the voice that is speaking in the text as Jesus, I figured it was just a metaphor.

I never, ever, in my wildest dreams thought Jesus would appear to me. He had to be mistaken. Just down the road was a little church full of people waiting for him to appear – he should have visited them. They were looking forward to his second coming; I was not.

There must be some mistake, I thought. But then, it happened again.

In my meditation, in my mind's eye, again I saw and heard Jesus say, **Rest in me**. Again, I saw myself falling into Jesus' hands.

I was incredulous. I did not speak to anyone about this experience, but something definitely felt different within my life. I noticed I felt a certain peace.

I was going through a rough time. My sister had had a brain aneurysm and my dad was dying of cancer. Plus, the recession had hit and I was losing a lot of money. Add it all up, and I was tired – bone tired.

Week after week, the inner visions continued. Jesus would appear over and over again, and his only words for me were the same: *Rest in me*. The message was on a constant repeat, like a broken record.

What could that mean? I thought. *What does he want me to hear, to do, to learn?*

I asked myself these questions on a daily basis as I really wasn't sure how I was supposed to rest in him. So, I searched my mind and played with the answers.

- Does it mean I need to stop working so hard?
- Does it mean I need to stop helping my family so much?
- Does it mean I need to come to him for a better quality of sleep?

My musings may seem funny, or even odd, but these visions were startling and disarming to me.

The visions continued for a year. Slowly, I learned to see Jesus as a friend. I took his hand. I began to walk with him. I began to visit him in a beautiful Mediterranean garden in my mind's eye. Eventually, I grew to know in my heart that if I took everything to Jesus and gave it to him, I could rest. I could feel the peace that passes all understanding. So, that was what I started to do.

I started to take everything to Jesus and let go of control. I knew he had answers that I did not. I stopped trying to find answers or fix things myself. I discovered I could hand it all over. What a relief!

What joy I found in those simple three words: *Rest in me.*

WHAT DOES *A COURSE IN MIRACLES* SAY ABOUT REST?

The conventional western thought is that we sleep to rest. *A Course in Miracles* turns this concept on its head and says we rest when we awaken to who we truly are. The course clarifies this by saying collectively, we are the one Son-of-God, created by God himself. So, we are what God is. We are perfect love.

Most of us cover up this essence with all kinds of problems, negative beliefs, and emotions. We reject the idea of God, and we believe we have to do it all ourselves. We believe we are the God of our own universe; in this way, we divorce ourselves from the help of universal forces. We look around and we feel weary of and frightened by all the chaos we see in the world.

Many of us literally do not know what we think. We just want to be loved and accepted, and so we accept what we are taught – even when it does not make sense to us. This is our dream; we are asleep because we have forgotten who we truly are. When we awaken to our true origin, we understand that we have never left God. God is within us, and we can and do have all the support we need. But first, we must believe this with conviction. We must have faith – not in the seen, but in the unseen. We must learn to trust what we know in our heart, and then the truth will resonate within us.

I found rest from the chaotic dream of my life when I finally stopped believing I had to do it all myself. When I learned I could give my problems over to the Christ within, or as some might what to say, to a higher power, I found true rest. I think this quote reflects what I found:

> *"Each hour that you take your rest today, a tired mind is suddenly made glad,*
> *a bird with broken wings begins to sing, a stream long dry begins to flow again.*
> *The world is born again each time you rest, and hourly remember that you came to bring*
> *the peace of God into the world, that it might take its rest along with you."*
> W, L109, 6:1-2

ALL YOUR TIME IS SPENT IN DREAMING

"All your time is spent in dreaming. Your sleeping and your waking dreams have different forms, and that is all. Their content is the same. They are your protest against reality, and your fixed and insane idea that you can change it."

T, 18, 5:12-15

THE SPECIAL ONES ARE ASLEEP: LOST IN DREAMS OF SPECIALNESS

"The special ones are all asleep, surrounded by a world of loveliness they do not see. Freedom and peace and joy stand there, beside the bier on which they sleep, and call them to come forth and waken from their dream of death. Yet they hear nothing. They are lost in dreams of specialness."

T, 24, III, 7:1-4

REST COMES FROM WAKING, NOT SLEEPING

"Rest does not come from sleeping but from waking. The Holy Spirit is the Call to awaken and be glad. The world is very tired, because it is the idea of weariness. Our task is the joyous one of waking it to the Call for God."

T, 5, II, 10:4-7

REST IN PEACE IS A BLESSING FOR THE LIVING

"'Rest in peace' is a blessing for the living, not the dead because rest comes from waking, not from sleeping. Sleep is withdrawing, waking is joining."

T, 8, IX, 3:5

I REST IN GOD

"'I rest in God.' This thought will bring to you the rest and quiet, peace and stillness, and the safety, and the happiness you seek."

W, L109, 2:1-2

FIND REST

"Many are called but few are chosen should be, 'All are called but few choose to listen.' Therefore, they do not choose right. The 'chosen ones' are merely those who choose to listen sooner. Right minds can do this now, and they will find rest unto their souls."

T, 3, IV, 7:12-16

REST IN HIS LOVE

"Rest in His Love and protect your rest by loving."

T, 7, VII, 6:4

Chapter 5

HEALTH: What Is Health?

Western Thinking
- Health is body wellness.

Reverse Thinking
- Health is inner peace.

Chapter 5 – Health: What Is Health?
Is health the absence of bodily sickness? *A Course in Miracles* teaches us that we are so much more than our bodies, and that while the body can be sick, the spirit never is. Find out what the course teaches us is the true source of our feelings of health.

bit.ly/healthwhatis

HEALTH IS INNER PEACE:
MY PERSONAL EXPERIENCE WITH THIS REVERSE THOUGHT.

I tell my clients in the marketing and advertising world, "Be prepared. Everyone gets a winter." It is just the cycle of nature at work. We get a spring. We get a summer. We get a fall. And just as surely, we get a winter.

MY WINTER
The year was 2006. My dad had been diagnosed with cancer and was fighting the disease. At the same time, my sister Jennifer, her husband, and their three kids had sold their house in the spring, but the new home they were building was not ready for them to move in. Consequently, they had moved in with my parents. My sister was sleeping on the floor in my parent's living room, her husband was sleeping in their new half-built house to protect it from vandals, and their children were sleeping in my parents' upstairs bedrooms.

That fall, the pressure of Jenny's three kids going back to school, her home not being completed, our dad's cancer, and the problems in her marriage pushed her stress levels right over the edge. Her brain literally popped; she had a brain aneurysm and ended up in the hospital.

The aneurysm was at the base of my sister's head, on her spinal cord, and it affected the whole left side of her body. She could not see, she was dizzy, and she was quite simply scared for her life. She had three young kids with multiple needs and no permanent home, and she could not get out of bed.

So, she came to live with me.

At this time, I was working towards setting up my business so it was not so dependent on me. My business support group said, "You need to learn to take your hands off the reins. Work on your business, not in your business." To do this, I hired an expensive marketing director to lead my company. I was going to follow my group's advice and settle more into the background, doing the writing and creating rather than being the sole person bringing in the business, handling the accounts, and writing all the creative. It was just too much.

That same winter, my dad's health seemed to get worse. He was told he was now terminal and may only have months to live. Life seemed dark and full of clouds.

Around this same time, I had a strange and beautiful dream.

CLEARING THE CLOUDS

I dreamed I met a First Nations chief who spoke to me clearly about my father. He was standing in front of a large screen, and when he waved his arm across it, pictures would appear.

Diane, he said. *Your father is at the end of his life, and this is what it looks like.* The screen filled with dark clouds. He cannot see what you can see. You are at the zenith of your life. He waved his arm in an arch and the scene shifted to show the sun shining brightly in the middle of the sky.

The man continued, *The end of life can be the most beautiful time of life – it is like a gorgeous sunset.* He waved and again the image changed to reveal a stunning multi-coloured sunset.

Your father cannot see this beauty. He is focused only on his body's health, or lack of it. He can not see his own beautiful sunset because he has covered it in clouds of confusion, pain, worry, doubt, anxiety, and sadness.

And with this, the picture on the screen was once again covered in dark clouds.

I need you to help your father remove the clouds of darkness and confusion from his vision. Help him see beyond the health of his body. Help him to see the beauty of his own sunset.

And with that, the screen again revealed the beauty of the setting sun, shining its golden rays out onto my face.

I awoke feeling the warmth of the dream, and I was clear about what I had to do. I had to help my father see beyond the illness in his body. I had to help my father see his own light and his own beautiful sunset. I had to help him remove the clouds of confusion, doubt, and worry from his mind. But how was I going to do that?

I turned within and asked the Holy Spirit for help. Inside of me, a voice said, *Take your father with you to Inspire Health.*

Inspire Health was a client I was working for at the time. I was in the process of rebranding their whole company with their new name, which meant changing their logo, signage, stationary, brochures, manuals, and everything related to their brand. It was a big project involving almost fifty separate promotional pieces. From working with this organization, I knew they offered a wonderful integrated health program for people dealing with cancer. This program introduced patients to Inspire Health's care philosophy, which focused on wholistic healthcare – bringing together the expertise of alternative, herbal, and traditional medicine. The program covered everything from daily food preparation and meditation to choosing between herbal and traditional medicines. Patients would take this program and then work with a variety of practitioners to promote healing, from massage therapists to medical doctors.

Inspired by their work and by my own internal urgings, I asked my dad if he was interested in going with me to Inspire Health.

He hung his head and slumped in his chair, saying he was nauseated and did not feel like seeing anyone. To say he was miserable and depressed would be an understatement. I left the topic alone for that day, but I didn't give up.

In the days that followed, I kept asking my father just to accompany me. I told him he could simply come for the ride and then sit in the waiting room while I met with the client. He could just get a feel for the place; he did not have to do anything. Plus, I added, they served this great Rooibos tea. They made a large urn of it every day and their clients, staff, family, and friends simply helped themselves. I told him he could pour himself a nice hot cup of tea and just look at the health care books in their quiet library, which served as their waiting room. After several invitations, he decided to accompany me one cold winter's day.

When we arrived, I met with the staff at Inspire Health and told them I had brought my dad to their office. I said he did not have the money to take their program, but I was wondering if they could help us out – any assistance would be appreciated. They said they would have to discuss it privately. I left them alone and went out to the library to wait and have a cup of tea with my dad.

Not long after, they came out to tell my dad and myself that they were going to let my dad do their program for free! I was delighted; my dad, well, not so much. But I knew this program and this place had the potential to change his life. I had seen it happen before.

Eventually, my dad went to the seminar and found people of all ages with cancer – even some in their teens. As a man in his seventies, he felt surprisingly lucky when he looked around the room. Everyone in the program talked about their own life stories and struggles. He saw how he had been blessed with a great family – children and grandchildren – and so many years to enjoy them. What about the teenagers in his program? They may never have children of their own, let alone grandchildren.

His judgments about his health and well-being had blocked his true inner knowledge about his life and his spirit in every way, but now the clouds started to slowly clear within his mind. He didn't feel so depressed, so unhappy, about having cancer. Instead of focusing on his disease and what was wrong with his life, he began to see what was right.

As my dad continued to go to Inspire Health, the clouds of his confusion started to lift as he began to give to others and see how rich his life had truly been. He did not feel bad for what he had; instead, he felt happy for all he had been given. His spirit was no longer blocked from his vision. Finally, he was aligned with the love and light within him. I know he felt great inner peace with what he had experienced, and he was suddenly grateful rather than depressed about his life.

Later, many people in this program told me that my dad was an amazing inspiration to them.

Throughout his time with Inspire Health, my dad began to lift his head and open his heart. Although he died just a few months later, he inspired those he met during this time. His body may have been sick, but he cleared his mind and found the peace he needed to be grateful and happy.

In the end, I knew my dad felt the golden rays of his own sunset.

WHAT DOES *A COURSE IN MIRACLES* SAY ABOUT HEALTH?

"The body cannot heal, because it cannot make itself sick. It needs no healing.
Its health or sickness depends entirely on how the mind perceives it,
and the purpose that the mind would use it for.
It is obvious that a segment of the mind can see itself
as separated from the Universal Purpose.
When this occurs the body becomes its weapon, used against this Purpose,
to demonstrate the 'fact' that separation has occurred.
The body thus becomes the instrument of illusion,
acting accordingly; seeing what is not there,
hearing what truth has never said and behaving insanely,
being imprisoned by insanity."

T, 19, I, 3:1-6

HEALTH OR SICKNESS DEPENDS ENTIRELY ON HOW THE MIND PERCEIVES IT

A Course in Miracles says health is inner peace because the body reflects our inner mindset. Some of this is unconscious. No one in their right mind would choose sickness, but there are parts of our mind that are not aligned with the right mind – the mind that thinks only from love.

The course says the body is a communication tool, and that sickness tells us there is a part of our mind that is still not at peace. We do not need to beat ourselves up when this occurs; rather, we need to love ourselves more. We were given eternal life, and we use the physical body to prove that we can die. However, the Holy Spirit knows you never die, you just transition from one state to another state. Your true nature is spiritual, not physical.

We need to treat our bodies with tender, loving care while we are here. When we do so, we align with the love that is our true essence. Then, even if we are in a "sickness process," we can experience inner peace within the physical body.

PAIN IS A SIGN ILLUSIONS REIGN IN PLACE OF TRUTH

"Pain is a sign illusions reign in place of truth. It demonstrates God is denied, confused with fear, perceived as mad, and seen as traitor to Himself. If God is real there is no pain."

W, L190, 3:1-2

IT IS YOUR THOUGHTS ALONE THAT CAUSE YOU PAIN

"It is your thoughts alone that cause you pain. Nothing external to your mind can hurt or injure you in any way. There is no cause beyond yourself that can reach down and bring oppression. No one but yourself affects you. There is nothing in the world that has the power to make you ill or sad, or weak or frail."

W, L190, 5:1-5

HEALTH IS UNITED PURPOSE

"The opposite of joy is depression. When your learning promotes depression instead of joy, you cannot be listening to God's joyous Teacher and learning His lessons. To see a body as anything except a means of communication is to limit your mind and to hurt yourself. Health is nothing more than united purpose."

T, 8, VII, 13:1-4

HEALTH IS INNER PEACE

"Health is inner peace. It enables you to remain unshaken by lack of love from without and capable, through your acceptance of miracles, of correcting the conditions proceeding from lack of love in others."

T, 2, I, 5:11-12

HEALTH RELINQUISHES ALL ATTEMPTS TO USE THE BODY LOVELESSLY

"Health is the result of relinquishing all attempts to use the body lovelessly. Health is the beginning of the proper perspective on life under the guidance of the one Teacher Who knows what life is, being the Voice for Life Itself."

T, 8, VIII, 9:9-10

"Spirit is in a state of grace forever. Your reality is only spirit.

Therefore you are in a state of grace forever.

T, 1, III, 5:4-6

WWW.DIANELUNDMIRACLES.COM

PART TWO

CONFLICT AND FEAR:
How to Survive the
Daily News

"The correction of fear is your responsibility.
When you ask for release from fear,
you are implying that it is not.
You should ask, instead, for help in the conditions
that have brought the fear about.
These conditions always entail a willingness to be separate.
At that level you can help it."

T, 2, VI, 4:1-5

 # INTRODUCTION

US VERSUS THEM

Years ago, I saw a photo of a car crash on the cover of our local newspaper. People had died in the crash, and I thought, *The daily news reports so many negative things. I do not want to hear about every awful thing that happens every day. What about all the beautiful things?* So, I cancelled my subscription.

This was my first conscious step toward stopping the ongoing horrors of the daily news from arriving into my personal space. However, that decision to stop bad news at the door did not stop any of the bad things happening out in the world. In essence, I was just lessening the number of times I ran into it.

When you watch the news, the world seems to be a battleground. Everyone is claiming that they know what is best and fighting with others to win their point, their land, their argument, or their right to protest.

To me, it looked like everyone in the world was picking sides – a world of us versus them.

I wondered, how can we do it differently? How can we turn around the violence, the hatred, and the willingness to go to war with families, companies, countries, and ourselves?

After years of studying *A Course in Miracles*, I believe we can start by facing our fears rather than fighting them.

FACING OUR FEARS

Ask yourself: What do I fear? Your answer might include:

- wild animals,
- getting lost,
- being alone,
- losing your job,
- losing people you love,
- losing your money, and more.

There are certainly as many fears as there are people.

To reinforce our fears, we take in a daily diet of the news. We get it on our cellphones as soon as we wake up. It is all over the internet, TV, billboards, social media, and print. And generally, it gives us a long list of bad things happening on our physical plane.

- Death
- Car accidents
- Getting lost
- People missing
- Shootings at schools and malls
- War zones
- Deadly diseases
- People losing limbs
- People battling with injustice

The list goes on and on. Occasionally there is a feel-good story, but for the most part, as they say in the media business, "if it bleeds, it leads." It's a daily onslaught.

In sharp contrast to what we see on our many screens or read in print, most of us have never seen a person get shot to death in front of us – thank goodness! It is a reality only in our mind's eye. Nevertheless, to combat all the troubles, dangers, and horrors we see or hear about, we are told to protect ourselves.

- Lock your doors
- Secure your car with a big metal stick
- Install a home alarm system
- Do not trust strangers
- Do not answer strange texts
- Guard yourself and your children
- Wear a helmet when you ride a bike or snowboard
- Buckle your seat belt when you are driving
- Read the labels on everything you eat
- Avoid white sugar and white flour
- And for heaven's sake, change those passwords – frequently!

When we need all these protections and defenses in our world, what we are really saying is that we believe all those awful images we see and hear about.

- We believe we can be hurt.
- We believe we can be killed.
- We believe people will hurt us.
- We believe we will get sick.

We believe that the negative, dark side of life has the power to take us down and take us out. It is negative thinking, and it is all based in fear.

WHAT IS WRONG WITH FEAR-BASED THINKING?

According to *A Course in Miracles*, when you think from fear you are aligning your thinking with your ego, or wrong-mindedness. The ego believes in separation, specialness, and death, and it is rooted in a foundation of fear. The body is the ego's biggest creation, and it seems to put a limit on eternal love.

"It is only the awareness of the body that makes love seem limited.
For the body is a limit on love.
The belief in limited love was its origin,
and it was made to limit the limitless."

T, 18, VIII, 1:1-3

"The body is a tiny fence
around a little part of a glorious and complete idea.
It draws a circle, infinitely small,
around a very little segment of Heaven,
splintered from the whole,
proclaiming that within it is your kingdom,
where God cannot enter."

T, 18, VIII, 2:5-6

Death of the body reinforces the ego's belief system that we are indeed separate from each other and separate from God. Physical death is real to us on the physical level; however, *A Course in Miracles* asks us to look beyond the physical to the level of the mind, and the level of the spirit.

When you align with right-minded thinking, you are not body-identified – you are spirit-identified. That does not mean you deny physical realities. Instead, it means that you come to understand that while your body can be killed, the real, authentic you – your eternal soul which is part of the one Son or one spirit – can never die.

To understand how to free ourselves from the daily barrage of bad news, which can trigger fear and persistent negative thinking, we must first be willing to look at how we create fear in the first place.

THE CORRECTION OF FEAR IS YOUR RESPONSIBILITY

The course says that the correction of fear is our responsibility, and it is our thinking that has brought it into existence.

A Course in Miracles says that the physical world is made through projected thoughts that come from our mind. This is not new concept. Quantum physics also says the physical world is an illusion, made of nothing but energy. Below is a quote from an article written by Lachlan Brown in 2018, called "Reality is an illusion: The scientific proof everything is energy and reality isn't real."

> *"Instead, as famous physicist Sir Roger Penrose theorized, we must envision the universe as nothing but information.*
>
> *We must believe that the physical universe is just a product of an abstract universe, in which we are all connected in an unobservable way.*
>
> *Information is simply embedded into the physical constructs of the physical universe, but is transmitted to our physical states from the abstract realm, first theorized by Greek philosopher, Plato.*
>
> *As Erwin Schrodinger famously stated, 'What we observe as material bodies and forces are nothing but shapes and variations in the structure of space. Particles are just appearances.'*
>
> *Simply put, everything is nothing but energy."*

Eastern mystics have also made this claim for thousands of years. If the world is an illusion we create through projected thought, we need to change our thoughts in order to change our physical reality.

However, the ego is extremely invested in you believing the complete opposite of this. The ego wants you to believe that the physical world is the cause of your fear, NOT that the physical world is the result of the fear in your mind. In fact, the whole world that we see is deeply invested in the belief that fear is out there in the world – outside of ourselves.

The daily news is just one way we reinforce this wrong-minded perception. We also do it by focusing on fearful thoughts rather than loving thoughts. Fear anchors duality into place. Without fear, there is ONLY love.

The next chapter looks at our divisions, splits, and fears to sees how we might turn them around to find a gentler, more peaceful path, both for ourselves and for generations to come.

 # Chapter 6

FEER: Where Is Fear Found?

Western Thinking
- Fear is in the world.

Reverse Thinking
- Fear is in my mind.

Chapter 6 – Fear: Where Is Fear Found?
Are there things out there to be frightened of? Or, does fear originate within each of us? What is the root of fear? Find out what answers *A Course In Miracles* gives for these questions.

bit.ly/whereisfear

FEAR IS IN OUR MIND:
MY PERSONAL EXPERIENCE WITH THIS REVERSE THOUGHT

The daily news seems to be dedicated to inciting fear. Almost every day we hear about people who have died, buildings that have caught on fire, cars that crashed, people who were ripped off, people who have a deadly disease or have COVID-19 and died. The news seems to dictate why we should be afraid – very afraid! In fact, sometimes I joke that the daily news could easily be called the "Daily Fear Report."

In many cultures, and for many people, it appears fear is running our communities and our lives. However, if we take a step back and look at the bigger picture – at the actual statistics on death and disease in the western world – we can see that generally speaking, we have never lived in safer times. For example, if you go back just a generation or two in most families in the western world, you will find that almost every family lost a child in childbirth or to a childhood disease. Today, you rarely hear about this. Sure, it still happens, but not as much as it did several decades ago. Today, we see it on the news because it is unusual.

My husband (who is now happily retired) was a Medical Health Officer, and part of his job was to review and analyze health statistics. He used to tell me, "We have never lived in more affluent and safer times."

Despite these facts, we still believe that awful things are happening in the world at an alarming rate – we believe fear is out there. Why, just the other day I heard a policeman state that the number of deaths in our community last year was significantly down from previous years. I found this surprising because we regularly hear about people being gunned down in the news. My perception was that death by gun violence was actually increasing in our city, but my perception was wrong!

A Course in Miracles believes fear is not in the world. It is not out there waiting to gun you down or take you down. Instead, fear lives in our minds, and we feed it every day by focusing on it.

Here is one of my personal stories where I learned first-hand that fear is in my mind.

FACING THE FEAR OF DEATH
Fear of death is very common. My dad had it, so once he was diagnosed with cancer, he asked me, "Diane, tell me again about your near-death experience. What did you see on the other side?"

I, of course, told him all about my experience, hoping it would help alleviate some of his fear. (You can read about it in Book I in the chapter entitled "DEATH: Do We Die?") When I repeated what I learned – that our physical bodies die, but our eternal spirit never dies – he said to me, "I just cannot believe it. I believe we come from dust and we return to dust."

I replied, "Dad, you can believe whatever you like – it is your right. But once you have a near-death experience, you can never take that away. It showed me that something exists beyond the physical. Something exists beyond my body. I learned that I will not die because I had a felt experience of existing, thinking, and feeling without my body. That knowledge is now written across my heart."

"I wish I could believe it," he said with a dejected sigh. "I always wondered how I would die, and now that I have cancer, I know the answer. But it is no comfort. It is just frightening to think everything will come to a sudden end. I will come to an end."

"Only your body will end," I said. "You will not end. You will go on. You will be alive and well in spirit."

My dad hung his head, and I could see my words were not convincing him of anything. He was a man of science. So, I tried another tactic. I told him to watch an amazing video series called *The Elegant Universe* by Brian Greene. The series takes you on a journey of thought and explores the realm of physics, starting with Newtonian physics and taking you right through to string theory. In one scene, it talks about the different dimensions of the universe being like a sliced loaf of bread. Our physical universe is one slice, but right beside it is another slice – another universe that we cannot see. The theory suggests we are all trapped on one slice of the universe, and that sometimes things leak through from one slice to another. I love visual metaphors, and this one is particularly wonderful in my opinion. It helped me talk to my dad about dying and its implication – about leaving this slice for another one.

I told him, "The best thing is, Dad, I believe it does not really matter that you do not believe in life after death, because truth is truth. You do not have to believe in gravity for it to apply to you. Gravity does not make exceptions for a baby or a ball. Gravity just exists on this physical plane. Drop the baby or the ball and they will both fall. There are no exceptions. It does not depend on what you personally believe.

"I think this is also true for spiritual laws," I continued. "Truth does not make exceptions. Truth is truth. It does not bend or alter. I believe the truth is that life is eternal on the level of spirit. From this viewpoint, I know you will be okay. Your body is not you. You are so much more than your body, and when you die you will know this too. There are no exceptions to the rule. I am sure of that."

"I hope you are right," he said quietly.

THE WORST DAY OF MY LIFE

No one wants to get THAT phone call – the one that says a loved one is near death – and yet here it was. When I picked up the phone that morning, I heard the words I dreaded: "Your dad is dying. Come to the hospital right now."

When the phone had rang, I was getting my Father's Day gifts ready to take up to the hospital. I was planning on spending my last Father's Day with my dad celebrating him, not watching him die.

My husband and I jumped in the car. It was the worst drive of my life. With every passing mile, I thought about how I was on my way to see my dad die – perhaps he was already lying dead in his room. I stared out the car window stunned, unhappy, and full of dread.

We arrived at the hospital to find my sister Jenny already at his bedside. I rushed to his side and grabbed his hand as he took his last breath. My mother stayed down at the base of the bed; I think she thought if she did not come too close, it would not happen.

She asked Jenny, "Is he gone?"

"Yes, he's gone," Jenny answered as she wiped his forehead.

I leaned over my dad and whispered to him, "We love you, Daddy," as both my sister and I held his hands and kissed him. "We are here Dad. You are loved."

When I looked up, I said to my sister, "I better go get the nurse."

I raced into the hallway as my brain was shouting at me, No, no, no! This can't be. When I got to the nurse's station I blurted out, "My dad has died. He's dead. He was supposed to stay alive until my sister got back. She is in Italy. This can't be. It can't be! He was going to live to see Lori!" I was not speaking these words; I was sobbing them out of my chest.

The nurse came out from behind the desk and put her arm around me. "This is for the best," she said, "It is better that it was quick."

"What?" I was incredulous. My mind was racing.
For the best? For who?
For her, maybe, but not for me.
Not for my sister, who is half a world away.
This is not for the best.
Who was she to tell me what is for the best?

I found no solace with the nurse, so I raced back to my dad's room. She followed us in and closed my dad's beautiful blue eyes, which were still wide-open in death.

She asked if we wanted to be alone with him. We did. We closed the flimsy hospital curtains around us, creating a little shrine. Together, we all held hands and prayed. We told our dad how much we loved him. We rubbed his arms, held his hands, and gave him our last kisses. Our last Father's Day kisses ever! It was heartbreaking.

My husband, my sister, and I then drove to my mother's house to gather as a family. When we arrived, one of my nephews came running out to sister Jenny's car and literally broke down in the driveway. He had not made it to the hospital in time to see his grandpa alive. He fell to his knees in grief and wept on the hard, black asphalt. "I didn't get to say goodbye," he wailed.

Watching his little body sobbing on the ground, all our hearts broke again. "The Lund Dam," as my father used to call it, literally burst open. We all started sobbing and holding each other. It was a gut-wrenching pain that left me gasping for breath. I knew my dad's death would hurt, but I did not know it would hurt this much.

The rest of the day went by in a blur. I cannot even remember what we all did. Perhaps I don't want to remember. I felt deep grief, and I just wanted out of this reality. I wanted this day to be over with, so it was a relief when it was time to go to sleep.

THE BEST NIGHT OF MY LIFE

That night, I was awakened by a bright red light shining high up in the corner of my bedroom. Intuitively, I knew it was my dad. How can that be? It did not make any sense – my dad as a strange, red light.

Frightened, I jumped up and out of bed and ran downstairs. My two miniature wire-haired dachshunds followed me and started to bark and howl. They instinctively knew that my dad was there.

Once I was downstairs, I tried to calm myself. Diane, you of anyone cannot be afraid of death. Go back upstairs and talk to your father. He has come to speak with you.

Bravely, I turned around and went back upstairs to see if the red light was still there. It was, hovering high up in the corner of the bedroom. I laid down on my bed and closed my eyes, and in my mind's eye I went to the red light in the corner of the room. In my mind, I asked, *Is that you, Dad?*

Yes, it is! I heard him proudly exclaim on the inner channel. *Diane, I know you tried to tell me what death was like when I was in my body, but I did not believe you. Now, I cannot believe I am experiencing this! Death is so much better than you ever described. I feel joyous. Best of all, they have given me a job right away. I am happy. I wanted you to know, I am happy.*

This time, the tears that ran down my face were ones of joy. I was thrilled.

I replied, *I am so glad, Dad. I am so happy you have found the truth. I promised it would not be different for you. Truth is truth. I love you.*

I opened my eyes, delighted to know my dad was still with me – just on another slice of bread-time!

We decided to wait to have the funeral until my sister Lori came back from Italy. Dad had told her to go despite his diagnosis, and she had asked us not to tell her if he died while she was away because there was nothing she would be able to do about it. So, we honoured her wishes and waited for her return.

We planned the funeral for July 7, 2007: 7-7-7. The number seemed significant. Seven is often thought of as the number of spirituality. In addition, it is my life-path number. It seemed fated that we would honour my dad on that special day. While we waited for my sister to return from Europe, we created slide shows of my dad's life and finalized the plans.

When at last my sister returned, she had a surprise for us. She said she already knew our dad had passed because he had come to see her in the form of a red light. Just like me, when she saw the light, she instantly knew it was him. He had come to say goodbye to her. She was so touched by her experience that she brought us each an Italian red glass heart to symbolize his light and his passing. I was amazed! What were the odds that my sister would have the same experience as me on the other side the ocean?

I had never heard of anyone's spirit manifesting after death as a red light, but my sister's experience confirmed my own. No matter how odd or weird it might be, we had both received the same type of communication from our dad, even though we were halfway around the globe from each other at the time.

We all wore our Italian red glass hearts around our necks at my dad's funeral. It was a symbol of what we all now know in our hearts: that there is nothing to fear. No one dies, we just lose the outer physical shell. Our real, authentic self – our spirit – lives on, just on another slice of the universe.

WHAT DOES *A COURSE IN MIRACLES* SAY ABOUT FEAR?

A Course in Miracles says the separation from God, or our collective detour into fear, involved the following steps:

> *"First, you believe that what God created can be changed by your own mind.*
> *Second, you believe that what is perfect can be rendered imperfect or lacking.*
> *Third, you believe that you can distort the creations of God, including yourself.*
> *Fourth, you believe that you can create yourself, and that the direction of your own creation is up to you."*
>
> T, 2, I, 1:9-12

How can we ever know that this is true? Personally, I have discovered the only way to know what is true and what is not is to look within yourself for answers.

How can we know we create fear? We have to look within and see the story we are telling ourselves that causes the fear to rise up within us. However, many of us don't want to do this because we fear what we do not know. It is so much easier to look outside of ourselves and think it is the world, the government, or our parents that cause our fear. But the world is the cause of our thinking – it is an illusion we are creating together. The source of the illusion is in our mind, so that's where we need to be looking.

> *"No one can escape from illusions unless he looks at them,*
> *for not looking is the way they are protected."*
>
> T 11, V, 1:1

FEAR IS AN ILLUSION

Fear is actually an illusion. *A Course in Miracles* states:
- the ego is a thought system of fear, while
- the Holy Spirit is a thought system based on love.

A Course in Miracles makes the following distinction: we miscreate when we think from fear, and we create when we think from love.

We are here on the planet to figure out how to stop miscreating – or, to say it another way, to stop creating illusions that scare us all. We are all free, innocent, and full of love and joy, but we cannot perceive this reality while our mind is full of fear that blocks the knowledge of the love within.

So, how do we get rid of fear?

First, we do not shrink away from looking at it. Second, we can start getting curious about what we believe and think, and why. Then, if we don't like the perceptions that result from these beliefs, we can forgive ourselves for thinking this way and choose to think about the situation again from a loving perspective. When this happens – when all of us think from love – the course tells us that the illusion of the physical world will disappear and we will experience heaven on earth. As the course says,

"Fear binds the world. Forgiveness sets it free."
W, L332

YOU ARE THE AUTHOR OF FEAR
"God is not the author of fear. You are. You have chosen to create unlike Him, and have therefore made fear for yourself. You are not at peace because you are not fulfilling your function."
T, 4, I, 9:1:3

YOU CAN NEVER CONTROL THE EFFECT OF FEAR YOURSELF
"You can never control the effect of fear yourself, because you made fear, and you believe in what you made. In attitude, then, though not in content, you resemble your Creator, who has perfect faith in His creations because He created them. Belief produces the acceptance of existence. That is why you believe what no one else thinks is true. It is true for you because it was made by you."
T, 1, VI, 4:2-6

ALL ASPECTS OF FEAR ARE UNTRUE
"All aspects of fear are untrue because they do not exist at the creative level and therefore do not exist at all."
T, 1, VI, 5:1

FEAR IS A MISPERCEPTION
"All fear is ultimately reducible to the basic misperception that you have the ability to usurp the power of God."
T, 2, I, 4:1

IN TRUTH THERE IS NOTHING TO FEAR
"In truth there is nothing to fear. It is very easy to recognize this. But it is very difficult to recognize it for those who want the illusion to be true."
W, L48, 1:3-5

FEAR IS A SURE SIGN YOU ARE TRUSTING IN YOUR OWN STRENGTH

"The presence of fear is a sure sign that you are trusting in your own strength. The awareness that there is nothing to fear shows that somewhere in your mind, though not necessarily in a place you recognize as yet, you have remembered God, and let His strength take the place of your weakness. The instant you are willing to do this there is indeed nothing to fear."

W, L48, 3:1-3

FEAR DOES NOT EXIST

"I have already indicated that you cannot ask me to release you from fear. I know it does not exist, but you do not. If I intervened between your thoughts and their results, I would be tampering with a basic law of cause and effect; the most fundamental law there is. I would hardly help you if I depreciated the power of your own thinking."

T, 2, VII, 1:2-5

THE CORRECTION OF FEAR IS YOUR RESPONSIBILITY

"The correction of fear is your responsibility. When you ask for release from fear, you are implying that it is not. You should ask, instead, for help in the conditions that have brought the fear about. These conditions always entail a willingness to be separate. At that level you can help it."

T, 2, VI, 4:1-5

FEAR CAN BE SELF-CONTROLLED

"Fear cannot be controlled by me, but it can be self-controlled. Fear prevents me from giving you my control. The presence of fear shows that you have raised body thoughts to the level of the mind. This removes them from my control, and makes you feel personally responsible for them. This is an obvious confusion of levels."

T, 2, VI, 1:4-8

FEAR IS NOT OF THE PRESENT

"Fear is not of the present, but only of the past and future, which do not exist."

T, 15, I, 8:2

 # Chapter 7

DEFENSE: Do I Need to Defend Myself?

Western Thinking
- To be safe, defend yourself.

Reverse Thinking
- To be safe, be defenseless.

Chapter 7 – Defense: Do I Need to Defend Myself?
Do we need to defend ourselves? Does it help us? What makes us feel safe? Find out what *A Course in Miracles* says about being defensive.

bit.ly/needdefense

TO BE SAFE, BE DEFENSELESS:
MY PERSONAL EXPERIENCE WITH THIS REVERSE THOUGHT

In a competitive world, we are taught to defend our positions – to stand our ground and fight for what we believe in. However, in *A Course in Miracles* (and in life) defense is rooted in fear, as you only defend something if you think something can be lost. And to continue the thought, if you think something can be lost, you believe in those that have and those that have not. This is not God's thinking; this is our own fear-based thinking.

What if we turn this thought 180-degrees on its head?
Instead of thinking: To be safe, I need to defend myself.
How about: To be safe, I need to be defenseless?

What a reverse thought! We are safe when we are defenseless? Really? How could that possibly be true?

Here on planet Earth, there is hunger, war, and crippling diseases. I am not asking you to deny the physical world. I am asking you to look beyond the physical level to the spiritual level – to the part of yourself that is whole and eternal.

This is what God knows about you: you are an extension of what he is, and he is whole, eternal, and changeless. He made you exactly what he is, so you have endless creative power and total infinite love. He knows you are complete and whole or "holy."

"In the creation, God extended Himself to His creations and imbued them with the same loving Will to create. You have not only been fully created, you have also been created perfect. There is no emptiness in you. Because of your likeness to your Creator you are creative. No child of God can lose this ability because it is inherent in what he is, but he can use it inappropriately by projecting. The inappropriate use of extension, or projection, occurs when you believe that some emptiness or lack of exists in you, and that you can fill it with your own ideas instead of truth."
T2, I, 1:2-7

To summarize, God knows we have everything because we are created from him, and he is everything. There is no lack, no imperfection, and nothing to defend because nothing can be lost. What an amazing thought.

We are extensions of this eternal love, and so we must be everything that God is. The fact that we do not believe this is not a reality to God, and it can only be a reality to us if we think with deprivation and scarcity as our root source. When we deny that God or love is our root source, we believe we can be lacking and be deprived of something.

Sadly – and I want to emphasize "sadly" – we say, "I know better than God," and we set out to prove or show people just how real our lack truly is. In this way, we literally prove to ourselves that we are indeed lacking. Here's how we do it:

- We choose to believe things can be taken from us.
- We believe we can be deprived.
- Therefore, we believe we must defend what is ours.
- We believe we must not let things be taken from us.

Many in the western world point to our bodies as proof that something can be taken from us. We point to the death of the body as the ultimate proof that we know more than God. Just look, there it is on the news every night: we can be destroyed! Our lives can be taken from us! Death exists! Therefore, we wrongly conclude that we must argue, we must stand up for ourselves, we must defend our lives. When thinking like this, people choose to build walls, lock doors, and carry guns or big sticks or an anger that will scare the world away.

In contrast, God's position – or love's position – is that there is nothing to defend because nothing can be taken from you. Your body may be taken from you, but not your eternal life. You are spirit. You are eternal. You are love. That is what you are here to learn.

I had a dream that illustrated this point to me.

SERVED BY THE DIVINE

In my dream, I was taken up and out of my bed. I was flying over the United States, and I was being shown top-secret places that the public did not know about. In these places, violent plots were being hatched. Everything was under tight lock-down, and I was surprised to learn that there were people planning deadly actions. It was not a good discovery. In fact, in this dream, I was horrified. But my dream quickly moved on.

Suddenly, I was flying high above New York and over many very tall buildings. I landed in an elevator and seemed to rise up and up. Finally, the doors of the elevator flew open and I stepped out into the main corridor. Just down the hall there seemed to be a lot of activity and laughter. I moved towards the party and into the room, where it appeared there were a lot people being instructed on what was going to happen to them in the near future. They were shown that the building would be on fire and that they could choose what they wanted to do. Everyone gathered around and discussed the many possibilities.

Some people said that they were going to jump out the window. Others said they would go down the stairs. Still others said they would stay and call their families. There seemed to be an air of excitement and joy. But the most amazing thing of all was that each person had their own personal angel serving their every need. Whatever the individual wanted, the angel delivered. It was awe-inspiring to watch as each angel extended kind, loving care and concern to the individual they were serving. I walked from person to person and noted that no one seemed to be upset. People talked about how they would go to their death like we might talk about deciding whether or not to go on a trip. The atmosphere was bright and lively. Everyone was talking and laughing with each other, and with their angel.

I awoke from the dream feeling amazed. The central message of the dream seemed to be that every person in the building was being served perfectly, even in death! I carried this amazement with me for days. I even wrote about it in my journal: *Everyone is perfectly served by the divine at all times.* The reality of the message was mind-blowing. But as the days wore on and the busyness of life took over, my dream faded.

THE DAY THE WORLD CHANGED

A few months later, my husband woke me up as he sat up in bed and declared, "The world has changed forever. Turn on the TV! The world will never be the same again!"

He was not kidding. It turned out he had been lying in bed listening to his radio through his earphones when he heard about the attacks on the World Trade Center. I, on the other hand, was totally confused. I had been dead asleep, and as I stumbled to consciousness, I thought, *What? We never watch TV in bed, especially in the mornings. Why is he acting so weird? What is happening?*

I will never forget the horror I felt as I saw a plane fly into the side of the World Trade Center. We could not believe what we were seeing; it just couldn't be true. Both of us watched in utter disbelief as one tower fell to the ground, and then the other. It was an unthinkable tragedy. It was clear that my husband was right: the world would never be the same again.

Later that day, as the horror played over and over again on the TV screen and everyone seemed to be walking around in a daze, I remembered my dream about a tower in New York. I remembered that in my dream the building was on fire, and that the people at the party were being shown their future and deciding how they would leave the burning building. I did not fully understand at the time that they were actually leaving the planet. With horror, I realized the people in my dream were choosing how they would die while angels attended their every need, bringing them drinks, food, and a consoling touch.

Questions flooded my brain:

- Could it be true? Could it be that we know what is going to happen before it happens, but we suppress this knowledge and send it to our unconscious mind?
- Do some of us choose on a spiritual level to go through events that would horrify us on a physical level?
- Do we choose to leave our families for a higher purpose?
- Are we always so beautifully served by angels?

I felt totally overwhelmed. I went to my journal and read the entry about my dream from a few months ago. Somehow, the thought of angels serving the people in the tower comforted me. I suddenly wanted the families who had lost loved ones to know that their brother, sister, daughter, son, husband, or wife was never alone. They did not fight their fate in my dream; they were happy and even seemed to embrace the event. They partied, laughed, and planned.

Looking back at my dream, those people were the embodiment of defenselessness. They knew that no matter what the event looked like on the physical level, they were being perfectly served by angels on the spiritual level. There was no fear in the room – in fact, I had felt a deep and profound love when I awoke from my dream which lasted for days.

What a reversal from the way we normally think: to even entertain the idea that I was shown a dream where love ruled, not fear, in one of the world's worst attacks. Of course, that is not what we saw on television. What we saw with our physical eyes was horror; what I saw with my spiritual inner vision was something completely different.

This dream, this vision, still haunts me today. I have wondered if sharing this dream would be a comfort to the families who lost loved ones. Of course, it depends on what they believe and what their personal perspective on life is, but perhaps some might find comfort in my vision.

It is my firm belief that even in our worst physical nightmares, our spirits do not die. Our bodies die, but who we are authentically lives on. I sincerely believe the divine serves us all – as the course says – even when it may seem like we are abandoned.

Did you know we can only see one percent of the light spectrum?

Perhaps there are angels who exist but are not physically visible to us. What if angels attended our physical transition from body identification to spirit identification, with great respect and great love?

BODIES DIE. SPIRIT LIVES ON.

When *A Course in Miracles* says there is no need to defend, it is talking on the level of the spirit and on the level of the mind, where all is one.

How can you defend against what you are?
If we are all one, how can one defend against one?

It is a metaphysical question, much like the Zen Buddhism koan, "What is the sound of one hand clapping?"

In spirit, we are all one mind. I have asked myself these questions:

- How can a mind stab itself?
- Why would the mind need to stab itself?
- Why would the mind need to defend against itself?

THE PHYSICAL WORLD IS TALKING ABOUT OUR PHYSICAL BODIES

When we look at the daily news, we see and hear about all the death and dying in the world. The ego likes this fear tactic because it proves its point: we are destructible, we are vulnerable, and we should be afraid – very afraid.

So, what do we do? After all, we are still here in bodies on the physical level. I believe a simple answer is that the course is not asking you to change anything on the physical, it is simply asking you to change your mind about who you truly are.

I believe that we try to do things backwards. We want everyone to put down their weapons of destruction while the idea of destruction still lives on in our minds.

I believe that even if everyone on the planet could get rid of all their weapons, we might just pick up a huge stone and hit someone over the head with it if we felt we were threatened. Safety does not live in the world or in behaviour; safety lives in the mind.

When we are defensive, we reinforce the idea that we are not safe. When we are defenseless, though, our behaviour says "there is nothing I need defend against because nothing can truly be taken from me." This is true safety – to know who you truly are, and that nothing can ever truly hurt you. This is what Jesus came to teach. You are love. You cannot be destroyed. You are not your body. You are life eternal.

In this loving mindset, there is no need for attack, no need to defend, for nothing can be lost or destroyed that is "real."

WHAT DOES *A COURSE IN MIRACLES* SAY ABOUT DEFENSE?

> *"We look past dreams today,*
> *and recognize that we need no defense because we are created unassailable,*
> *without all thought or wish or dream in which attack has any meaning.*
> *Now we cannot fear, for we have left all fearful thoughts behind.*
> *And in defenselessness we stand secure, serenely certain of our safety now,*
> *sure of salvation; sure we will fulfill our chosen purpose,*
> *as our ministry extends its holy blessing through the world."*
> W, L153, 9:1-3

I am not advocating that you do not lock your doors or take the physical precautions that you need to in this moment. Instead, I am asking you to consider going beyond the physical to allow your spiritual sight to see that you are eternal, and as eternal spirit, your true essence can never be hurt or destroyed. Many, unfortunately, believe we die, but *A Course in Miracles* counters this viewpoint with the following statement:

> *"You can wait, delay, paralyze yourself,*
> *or reduce your creativity almost to nothing,*
> *but you can not abolish it."*
> T, 1, V, 1:5

In other words, it is up to you. You are one hundred percent safe in spirit, but if you do not believe you are safe, you will attack, defend, and destroy in the name of safety. However, if you change your identification from body to spirit, you will understand that on the level of spirit, there is nothing to defend. From this perspective, defenselessness is the answer. It is such a huge reversal of thought. Think on this:

> *"Everyone defends his treasure, and will do so automatically.*
> *The real questions are, what do you treasure,*
> *and how much do you treasure it?"*
> T, 2, II, 2:4-5

To become defenseless, we must know in our heart of hearts that we can never be destroyed or hurt. This is the knowledge Jesus possessed when he went to his death without arguing with the courts. He knew the world was an illusion, and that all that is to be done is to forgive what was never real and return to love. This is what he says the crucifixion demonstrates:

"Teach only love for that is what you are."

T 6, I, 13:2

"Assault can ultimately be made only on the body.
There is little doubt that one body can assault another, and can even destroy it.
Yet if destruction itself is impossible, anything that is destructible cannot be real.
Its destruction, therefore, does not justify anger.
To the extent to which you believe that it does,
you are accepting false premises and teaching them to others.
The message the crucifixion was intended to teach
was that it is necessary to perceive any form of assault in persecution,
because you cannot be persecuted.
If you respond with anger,
you must be equating yourself with the destructible,
and are therefore regarding yourself insanely."

T 6, I, 4:1-7

NO ONE ATTACKS WITHOUT INTENT TO HURT

"No one attacks without intent to hurt. This can have no exception. When you think that you attack in self defense, you meant that to be cruel is protection; you are safe because of cruelty. You mean that you believe to hurt another brings you freedom."

W, L170, 1:1-4

THE WORLD PROVIDES NO SAFETY

"The world provides no safety. It is rooted in attack, and all its 'gifts' of seeming safety are illusory deceptions."

W, L153, 1:2-3

ATTACK, DEFENSE; DEFENSE, ATTACK, BECOME THE CIRCLES

"Attack, defense; defense, attack, become the circles of the hours and the days that bind the mind in heavy bands of steel with iron overlaid, returning but to start again. There seems to be no break nor ending in the ever-tightening grip of the imprisonment upon the mind."

W, L153, 3:2-3

DEFENSE MAKES FEAR REAL

"Defense is frightening. It stems from fear, increasing fear as each defense is made. You think it offers safety. Yet it speaks of fear made real and terror justified."

W, L135, 3:1-3

DEFENSES ARE PLANS AGAINST THE TRUTH

"Defenses are the plans you undertake to make against the truth. Their aim is to select what you approve, and disregard what you consider incompatible with your beliefs of your reality."

W, L135, 17:1-3

THE BEST DEFENSE IS TO NOT ATTACK BUT PROTECT THE TRUTH

"The best defense, as always, is not to attack another's position, but rather to protect the truth."

T, 3, I, 2:1

IN MY DEFENSELESSNESS I WILL BE STRONG

"If I defend myself I am attacked. But, in my defenselessness I will be strong and I will learn what my defenses hide."

W, L135, 22:4

WITHOUT DEFENSES YOU BECOME A LIGHT

"Without defenses, you become a light which Heaven gratefully acknowledges to be its own. And it will lead you on in ways appointed for happiness according to the ancient plan, begun when time was born. Your followers will join their light with yours, and it will be increased until the world is lighted up with joy. And gladly will our brothers lay aside their cumbersome defenses, which availed them nothing and could only terrify."

W, L135, 20:1-4

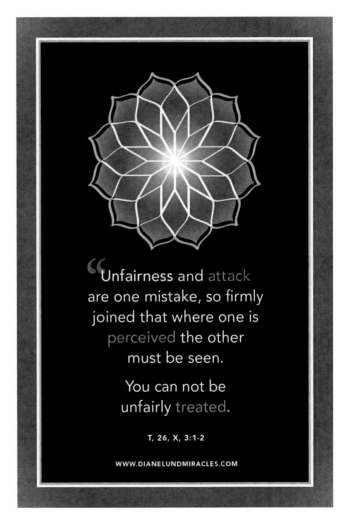

"Unfairness and attack are one mistake, so firmly joined that where one is perceived the other must be seen.

You can not be unfairly treated.

T, 26, X, 3:1-2

WWW.DIANELUNDMIRACLES.COM

Chapter 8

ANGER: Is My Anger Justified?

Western Thinking
- Anger is justified.

Reverse Thinking
- Anger is never justified.

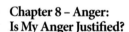

Chapter 8 – Anger: Is My Anger Justified?
Do you lose your temper? *A Course In Miracles* teaches us to question anger and whether it is justified. It asks us to question whether we can ever truly lose anything if we are whole and complete spiritually. Anger never solves problems – it creates them. Find out why and how in this video.

bit.ly/angerjustify

ANGER IS NEVER JUSTIFIED:
MY PERSONAL EXPERIENCE WITH THIS REVERSE THOUGHT

According to *A Course in Miracles*, all anger is a call for help, and that it is NEVER justified – isn't that an amazing statement! Here's the full quote:

> *"Anger is never justified. Attack has no foundation.*
> *It is here escape from fear begins, and will be made complete.*
> *Here is the real world given in exchange for dreams of terror."*
>
> T, 30, VI, 1:1-4

ANGER IS NEVER JUSTIFIED?

I can just hear the questions you might be asking.

- What if a drunk driver kills my child?
- What if an earthquake destroys my home?
- What if my partner cheats on me?
- What if my business partner gambles away all the company money?

The course is abundantly clear: anger is never justified on the level of the mind.

On the physical level, anger is a response that comes up to alert us that we are hurting ourselves. When we scream or yell at someone, they might feel hurt or they might not. But no matter how they react, one thing is totally clear: your peace has been disturbed, and you are suffering. **You are hurting yourself!** But often we do not acknowledge this fact. Instead, we believe our anger helps.

Why?

Our deeply hidden belief is that our anger is justified because we believe we are separated from our brothers and sisters, and that they are hurting us. But the real truth is that **we are hurting ourselves**! This statement bears repeating: **we are hurting ourselves when we get angry.**

ROAD RAGE

Imagine for a moment that you are in the front passenger seat of a car and your partner is driving in the fast lane. The truck in front of you is going too slowly for your partner, so they get mad and yell at the truck.

Question: Who is the yelling hurting?

Does the person in the truck ahead of you hear your partner yelling? In most cases, the answer is no.

The person yelling mistakenly believes that getting their misery out into the world will make the world change. But the world does not change when you yell at it, much like a computer screen does not change when you yell at it. In fact, the world is really the screen of our one collective mind.

SO, WHAT CAN WE DO?
Whatever you are seeing, you can decide to see something else. You can turn your focus from your physical vision to your spiritual vision.

You must acknowledge that you choose to see things like hurt, destruction, chaos, drama, and cheating. No one else is deciding to see this but you, and you are deciding to see this because you believe you are separate from other people and that they can hurt you. But what if the decision to hurt was really in your mind?

Seeing two bodies that can hurt each other may be your physical reality, but it is not God's reality. On the level of the physical form, anger need not be judged as bad – it can be helpful in alerting you to the fact that you are not comfortable with seeing things as they are, acting as a signpost to help you move in another direction. On the level of the mind, though, anger is not justified because nothing has changed within the eternal reality of love and peace.

God's reality is never about anything separated or anything that changes. God's world is eternal and unchanging. God is always one with everything and in perfect love. So, if we are one with God, it makes sense that we are perfect love too.

WHERE IS THIS ONENESS? WHERE IS THIS PERFECT LOVE?
Looking around, most people do not see the oneness of the world through their physical eyes. To see oneness, we must forgive what we are seeing with our physical sight. This requires us to use our spiritual sight and acknowledge that unloving actions are a call for love. When we shift our perception from outward looking to inward looking, we can acknowledge that we are all connected within the one mind.

ATTACK HAS NO FOUNDATION
If we are all eternal love, how can love attack love? The answer is clear: perfect love never attacks. If it did, it would not be perfect love.

The course teaches that attack has no foundation, and that is because the course aims to teach you how to be in alignment with God. You cannot be in accordance with God and attack. Perfect love does not attack;

therefore, attack has no foundation in what is real. And remember what the course says: what is real is only that which lasts eternally.

WHAT SHOULD I DO, JUST LIE DOWN AND TAKE IT?

We attack because we have an ego thought system in our mind that makes us see a world of separation, sin, guilt, and fear. To heal our belief that we are separate from God and are therefore NOT love, we have to heal our one mind's thought system. The way we do that is to forgive what we see out in the physical world, knowing that it is an illusion projected from our mind. It is not real, and therefore can be forgiven and changed if you go to the real source of the problem – a solution that is not out in the world, but rather is in our one collective mind. The course would say we are actually forgiving what never happened, which is a very different understanding of forgiveness than the traditional western definition.

THIS SEEMS LIKE A VERY BIG TASK.

Let's start with a small step: let's get curious and start with ourselves. *A Course of Miracles* says:

> *"All your difficulties stem from the fact*
> *that you do not recognize yourself, your brother or God.*
> *To recognize means to 'know again,' implying that you knew before.*
> *You can see in many ways because perception involves interpretations,*
> *and thus means that it is not whole or consistent.*
> *The miracle, being a way of perceiving, is not knowledge.*
> *It is the right answer to a question, but you do not question when you know.*
> *Questioning illusions is the first step in undoing them.*
> *The miracle, or the right answer corrects them."*
>
> T 3, III, 2:1-7

The first small step is to begin questioning what you think you know. Look around yourself; perhaps things are not what they seem to be. For centuries, wise men in the east have said that we live in an illusion or what they call "maya." Similarly, the course says everyone makes the world they see. Once you start to question whether there might be more than what you see on the surface, you begin to open your mind.

IF YOU HAVE TROUBLE, BE GENTLE WITH YOURSELF

If it seems impossible to question what you know, be gentle with yourself. The ego is deeply invested in maintaining your attack thoughts in order to reinforce the illusion that there is something outside of ourselves that is hurting us – to reinforce the belief in separation. If you simply notice this and do not judge it, you can begin to feel compassion for yourself. And once you feel compassion for yourself, it is easier to look outward with loving eyes rather than judging, condemning eyes.

If you want to live in a world of love rather than in a world of anger and hate, you have a choice to make: you must choose either the belief in separation or the belief in oneness and love. You cannot have it both ways; you cannot ride two horses that are going in opposite directions. You either ride the horse of love, or you ride the dark horse of fear and attack. Trying to ride both horses at once is what creates level confusion.

WHAT IS LEVEL CONFUSION?

According to *A Course in Miracles*, level confusion is when we want the principles of one level (spirit) to manifest in another level (physical). We quite literally want heaven here on earth. But we cannot have both heaven and earth, because by their very nature they contradict each other. Heaven is just eternal love; it is one thing. In contrast, Earth is a dualistic plane, always composed of the two things – up and down, night and day, right and wrong. So, just one thing can not exist in duality by its very nature. When we want both to be true, we create a split mind. In order to return to oneness, wholeness, holiness, we have to choose heaven or love and nothing else. Ask yourself the following:

Do you want to live your life based on the principles of love?
Or,
Do you want to live your life based on the principle of fear?

It is a question of knowing completely and truly who you are. You are, at your essence, love. You can choose to know this, and it is a choice only you can make. Ultimately, you must choose love no matter what is happening around you.

This does not mean that you deny the physical – instead, you forgive the physical and look deeper. Use not your eyes but your spiritual sight to see that everyone comes from the same source: love. Either they are love, or their bad behaviour is a call of love. They are hurting, and so they do not need more hurt. They need to be shown another way – the way of love.

The way the majority of people are prone to thinking is leading them into a dream of terror. When problems emerge, when fights happen, when chaos and anger erupt, someone must be saner in the present moment. Amidst the fear, anger, and attack, someone must choose to see beyond the surface and then actively demonstrate love. This is one way out. This is grace.

"Grace is the acceptance of the Love of God
within a world of seeming hate and fear."
W, L169, 2:1

WHAT DOES *A COURSE IN MIRACLES* SAY ABOUT ANGER?

Everyone has gotten angry; it is a human emotion. Anger flares up and alerts us we are not in accordance with the Holy Spirit's right-minded thinking – when we are thinking not from love, but from fear. We are angry deep down (unconsciously for most) because we believe we are separate from our brothers and sisters, and that one of them has done something we are choosing to hurt ourselves with. We then want to project our hurt and anger out on to the world, the person, the institution, or whatever we deem has destroyed our peace.

But ask yourself this: has angry behaviour ever brought more peace?

Looking at the history of the world, I would say that anger has never worked out in the long term. Getting your anger out may make you feel better in the moment, but it does not ultimately solve the problem because the problem is not out there. The problem is in our minds, in how we see the world. The problem is the separation we feel from our authentic nature – eternal love.

A Course in Miracles says we can heal separation through its specific form of forgiveness or pardon:

> *"Pardon is always justified. It has a sure foundation.*
> *You do not forgive the unforgivable,*
> *nor overlook a real attack that calls for punishment.*
> *Salvation does not lie in being asked to make unnatural responses*
> *which are inappropriate to what is real.*
> *Instead, it merely asks that you respond appropriately*
> *to what is not real by not perceiving what has not occurred.*
> *If pardon were unjustified, you would be asked to sacrifice your rights*
> *when you return forgiveness for attack.*
> *But you are merely asked to see forgiveness*
> *as the natural reaction to distress that rests on error, and thus calls for help.*
> *Forgiveness is the only sane response.*
> *It keeps your rights from being sacrificed."*
> T, 30, VI, 2:1-9

ANGER IS NEVER JUSTIFIED. ATTACK HAS NO FOUNDATION.

"Anger is never justified. Attack has no foundation. It is here escape from fear begins and will be made complete. Here is the real world given in exchange for dreams of terror. For it is on this forgiveness rests and is but natural. You are not asked to offer pardon where attack is due and would be justified. For that would mean that you forgive a sin by overlooking what is really there. This is not pardon. For it would assume that, by responding in a way which is not justified, your pardon will become the answer to attack that has been made. And thus, is pardon inappropriate, by being granted where it is not due."

T, 30, VI, 1:1-10

ATTACK IS ALWAYS MADE ON STRANGERS

"Attack is always made upon a stranger. You are making him a stranger by misperceiving him, and so you cannot know him."

T, 3, III, 7:3

IF YOU ATTACK WHO GOD LOVES YOU ARE NOT YOURSELF

"If you attack who God would heal and hate the one He loves, then you and your Creator have a different will. Yet if you are His Will, what you must then believe is that you are not yourself."

T, 22, I, 2-3

ATTACK MAKES ILLUSIONS REAL TO YOU

"Attack has power to make illusions real. Yet what it makes is nothing. Who could be made fearful by a power that can have no real effects at all? What could it be but an illusion, makings things appear like to itself."

T, 30, IV, 5:5-8

MY ONE LESSON

"My one lesson, which I must teach as I learned it, is that no perception that is out of accord with the judgment of the Holy Spirit can be justified. I undertook to show this was true in an extreme case, merely because it would serve as a good teaching aid to those whose temptation to give in to anger and assault would not be so extreme. I will with God that none of His Sons should suffer."

T, 6, I, 11:5-7

ATTACK IS ALWAYS PHYSICAL

"Attack is always physical. When attack in any form enters your mind you are equating yourself with a body, since this is ego interpretation of the body."

T, 8, VII, 1:1-2

WHOEVER IS SANER AT THE TIME

"Whoever is saner at the time the threat is perceived should remember how deep is his indebtedness to the other and how much gratitude is due him, and be glad that he can pay his debt by bringing happiness to both. Let him remember this, and say:

I desire this holy instant for myself,
that I may share it with my brother, whom I love.
It is not possible that I can have it without him, or he without me.
Yet it is wholly possible for us to share it now.
And so, I choose this instant as the one to offer to the Holy Spirit,
that His blessing may descend on us, and keep us both in peace."

T, 18, V, 7:1-6

Chapter 9

ACCIDENTS: Are There Accidents?

Western Thinking
- Accidents happen.

Reverse Thinking
- Nothing is an accident.

Chapter 9 – Accidents: Are There Accidents?
Fire, car crashes, injuries… these are events that most people would call accidents. *A Course in Miracles* turns the concept of accidents on its head by showing us that there is NO SUCH THING. Watch the video to find out what the course teaches us about accidents.

bit.ly/accidentsare

NOTHING IS AN ACCIDENT:
MY PERSONAL EXPERIENCE WITH THIS REVERSE THOUGHT

KAUAI CRASH

My husband and I have gone to Kauai every other year for decades. We love the relaxed vibe of the island, and we have been there so often we have a bit of a routine. The first morning, we always get up and go to the Kauai Coffee Company to buy coffee for our trip. This is an amazing place where you can sample all the coffees they create, buy souvenirs, and walk around the coffee plantation.

On this particular trip, the usual route we take was blocked by construction, so we were rerouted down a large hill. We came to a stop behind two cars, the first of which was turning left. Suddenly, without any warning, a large disposal truck crashed into the back end of our small rental car, then slid across the road and took out another car going in the opposite direction. I was totally unprepared for the hit as I had not seen him coming. Cars stopped all around and people emerged to help us. Miraculously, no one was hurt.

We got out of the car and the driver of the truck immediately said, "I am so sorry. I just was not paying attention."

My husband responded, "Yes, I saw you coming in the rear-view mirror and you were looking down like you were texting."

Surprised, I asked my husband, "Why didn't you say something to me when you saw the truck in the mirror?"

He answered, "It all happened too fast. I could not believe what I was seeing. I thought surely he was going to stop until he drove right into the back of us."

The truck driver replied to my husband, "When I looked up, I realized my truck was so huge and your car so small that if I drove right into the back of you my truck would probably go right on top of your car and crush you. I did the best I could in the circumstances and turned the steering wheel as hard as I could into the oncoming traffic. That's why I hit the other car."

The man then collapsed on the ground in a heap and put his head in his hands and started to sob. He was visibly shaking. Everyone was in shock.

Reporting the whole incident to the required parties was not easy. We called the police, the rental company, and the insurance company. The rental company said they were going to call for a tow truck to come pick us up, along with the damaged car. Unfortunately, that is not what happened. Instead, we began a long, hot wait on the side of the highway. A kind Hawaiian woman waited with us as we all baked in the sun.

The crash happened around ten o'clock in the morning. At one in the afternoon, we were still waiting on the side of the road for the tow truck, getting completely burnt by the midday sun. We had not put on any sunscreen, nor brought any, because we thought we were just going out for a quick coffee.

As it turned out, there was a big mix-up. The rental car company was supposed to send a tow truck, but the truck was cancelled. The tow truck informed the rental company that they do not come to accidents, but someone forgot to relay this message to us. Consequently, we stood for hours, baking on the side of the highway. Eventually, we thanked the woman for her kind aloha spirit and told her she did not need to stay.

As fate would have it, a local Samaritan had seen us and the damaged cars on the side of the road when he was heading into town that morning, shortly after the accident happened. Hours later, he saw us still standing there on his way back from town, and he generously circled back to help us. As a local mechanic, he was able to wire up our car's bumper so we could drive the car back to the rental company. Truly, he was a godsend. Later, at the car rental dealership, they explained to our red and burnt faces that they were deeply apologetic for not giving us better service and leaving us out on the side of the road for hours. They offered us any car on the lot for the same price as our now destroyed little car, so we took the biggest car we could find and drove back to our condo, just thankful to be alive.

That night, I sat on the deck and watched the stars come out. I saw a shooting star streak across the sky, and I said a silent prayer of gratitude that everyone was safe and not in the hospital or dead. I truly believe the truck driver saved our lives by turning into the oncoming traffic. The car he hit was also destroyed, and it is a miracle no one in that car was hurt either.

The next day, I was sitting around the pool and began reading Mitch Albom's book The Timekeeper, which is about the man who invented time. It was an interesting choice because I had been thinking a lot about time since the crash – about how my husband's and my time on this planet could have been up yesterday.

The big question I asked myself was, *How would I feel if I had died yesterday?*

To my surprise, I did not feel badly about it. I knew all my relationships with the people I love were in good order, and that I had said all I wanted and needed to say. The only thing I did not feel good about was the fact that I was writing this book and it was not finished.

There are no accidents.

I believe I was in that car crash at that time in order to remind me that time is fleeting on this physical plane. I will not always be here in this body. So, if writing this book felt important and unfinished, I needed to get on with the job of finishing it. So, I gave silent thanks to the man in the large pink dump truck. I am sure the crash was something he needed, and something I needed too.

After all, I truly believe there are no accidents.

If everything in the universe works for my good and the good of the whole, I could see the beauty in my car crash. I was not in the hospital. I was not dead. I was alive, and more motivated than ever to finished what I started.

WHAT DOES *A COURSE IN MIRACLES* SAY ABOUT ACCIDENTS?

I believe everyone could write their own life story from two perspectives. One perspective would be to write down all the terrible things that had happened to them or that they had witnessed. The second perspective would be to write about the very same events and how they motivated them to change for the better. It is a fascinating exercise, and it is one I encourage you to try.

This book is asking you to turn the experience of your world upside down so you can get your life right side up. It is asking you to shift your mindset – in this case, it is asking you to move away from believing in accidents and living in a world of victims and casualties. In fact, many health organizations have decided there are no car accidents; instead, they refer to them as car crashes. Accidents imply victims while crashes acknowledge that someone is responsible.

We are all responsible for what we see. We could see a world full of victims and accidents, or we can choose to take back our God-given power. *A Course in Miracles* asks you to see events in the world using your internal spiritual vision. Here is one passage on the subject:

"Spiritual vision literally cannot see error, and merely looks for Atonement.
All solutions the physical eye seeks dissolve.
Spiritual vision looks within and recognizes immediately
that the altar has been defiled and needs to be repaired and protected.
Perfectly aware of the right defense it passes over all others,
looking past error to truth.
Because of the strength of its vision, it brings the mind into its service.
This re-establishes the power of the mind and
makes it increasingly unable to tolerate delay,
realizing that it only adds unnecessary pain.

T, 2, III, 4:1-6

NO ACCIDENT OR CHANCE IS POSSIBLE WITH THE UNIVERSE

"It is impossible the Son of God be merely driven by events outside of him. It is impossible that happenings that come to him were not his choice. His power of decision is the determiner of every situation in which he seems to find himself by chance or accident. No accident nor chance is possible with the universe as God created it, outside of which is nothing."

T, 21, II, 2:3-4

REMEMBER THAT NO ONE IS WHERE HE IS BY ACCIDENT

"Remember that no one is where he is by accident, and chance plays no part in God's plan."

M, 9, 1:3-4

YOU DO NOT WALK ALONE. GOD'S ANGELS HOVER NEAR AND ALL ABOUT.

"You do not walk alone. God's angels hover near and all about. His Love surrounds you, and of this be sure; that I never leave you comfortless."

W, Epilogue, 6:7-8

"Holding grievances is an attack on God's plan for salvation.

W, LESSON 72

WWW.DIANELUNDMIRACLES.COM

Chapter 10

PEACE: Where Is It?

Western Thinking
- Peace is something to seek.

Reverse Thinking
- Peace is revealed.

Chapter 10 – Peace: Where Is It?
Where is Peace? In nature? In beauty? In religion? *A Course In Miracles* explains that Peace is not something to seek, it is revealed. Find out how by watching the video.

bit.ly/wherepeace

PEACE IS REVEALED:
MY PERSONAL EXPERIENCE WITH THIS REVERSE THOUGHT

Peace is such a big topic, yet while many people would say that they want world peace, they are unable to find peace in their own lives. I think many of us look beyond ourselves for peace. We say, "When COVID ends, when the war in the Middle East ends, when the race war ends, when the drug wars end, then there will be peace." However, we do not turn and look at how we create war and conflict in our own lives.

If we really want peace, I believe we need to start in our own backyards. The question is, where do you lose your peace?

I think most people can relate to the idea that our family members are often our biggest obstacles to peace. We have thoughts like:
- I hate the way my mom relies on me to drive her everywhere.
- I hate that my brother and sisters do not take their turn hosting family dinners.
- I think my uncle does not treat our family members fairly – he picks favourites.

Personally, I know that my relationships with family members are where I need to learn and practice peace. In order to find more peace in our family, I may consider a number of external triggers:
- If only my mother would stop making demands of me.
- If she would just not create drama all the time.
- If she would just make up her mind.
- If she could just learn to share.

These kinds of statements or thoughts are all outward wishing, and in my experience, wishing has never changed anything.

Growing up in an alcoholic family, yelling and shouting were commonplace – we were like the loud family on Saturday Night Live. My dad's anger kept everyone dancing on eggshells every time he came home drunk. My siblings and I all knew we would be up late listening to our parents yelling and screaming. Everyone just seemed so hot-headed and ready to blow their top. Living there felt dangerous.

There was also an unspoken household rule that children should be seen and not heard. So, my siblings and I did not speak up or out easily, and we did not bother our parents unless there was some big problem that justified asking for help. I learned to frame my questions in the form of a problem if I wanted my parents to give me the time of day – if I did not have a problem, I did not get attention.

When I finally moved out of my parent's home, I was surprised to notice that other young people did not have problems all the time!

- What if I looked at things like they did?
- What if I changed my mind and allowed myself to start framing the world differently?

I really was not sure how to get this scarce commodity called peace, but I thought it might be worth the effort. After some thought, I decided that if I wanted peace, I needed a life that was not filled with problems and conflict.

First, I thought that intensifying my spiritual journey might finally deliver me at peace's door. Ironically, I found that many people on a spiritual path had just as many problems as anyone else. They did not seem more peaceful.

Next, I considered meditation – maybe that would work. But while meditation did calm my mind, it didn't get me to where I wanted to be.

In the end, peace came to me in miraculous ways.

FAMILY DAY

One year, on the Canadian holiday Family Day, my sisters and I decided that as a present to my mother, we would go over to her house and help her with some chores. At this time, my mother was in her eighties and quite crippled, with bad knees and hips. She had difficulty walking around her home, which had many stairs connecting three levels.

For years, my sisters and I had been wondering how to get our mother to live in a safer place. We all imagined that she would fall down the stairs and lay there for days before she was found. We worried she could no longer clean her house or look after her yard and property. However, we also acknowledged she was not yet ready to leave her home. So, we decided to help her clean up her basement suite, thinking that perhaps she could make some extra income off of it so she could hire people to help her around the house.

My sister and I knew that helping my mom clean her basement would not be an easy job as she does not like to throw anything out. We knew we would likely have a fight on our hands, and we were right. No matter what we were sorting through – old magazines, books, Dad's fishing gear, Christmas decorations, dishes, furniture, Dad's old rolled-up architectural drawings – she wanted to control everything we touched. I found the situation very trying on my patience, but I was determined not to attack or fight.

Then, the moment to test my resolve arrived.

TRUE FORGIVENESS: A THOUGHT PROCESS EXAMPLE

I was moving a large sheet of copper out of the way when my mother came up and got right in my face. She yelled at the top of her lungs, "Do not touch that piece of copper! It is extremely valuable, and thieves will probably break into the house and steal it."

She wanted the copper sheet covered up. "Right now!" she screamed, her face growing redder and redder.

She was so angry and so close that I suddenly started to watch her mouth move. Her voice seemed to fade away and I stood transfixed, watching her face move as if the soundtrack of the moment had disappeared.

I began mentally reciting a quote my ministry group had been practicing from Gary R. Renard's book, *The Disappearance of the Universe*:

> *You're not really there.*
> *If I think you are guilty or the cause of a problem,*
> *And if I made you up,*
> *then the imagined guilt and fear must be in me.*
> *Since the separation from God never occurred,*
> *I forgive "both" of us for what we haven't really done.*
> *Now there is innocence and I join with the Holy Spirit in peace.*
>
> P. 256

Suddenly, I saw my mom as a ball of white light and love. As I stared at her, no longer hearing her voice, she suddenly stopped yelling. Her mouth stopped moving. She looked straight into my eyes, and I knew she felt what I was experiencing. I could see she was feeling the love surrounding us, even if just for a second.

It was miraculous. I was no longer judging my mother's yelling. I was looking beyond her yelling to who I know she truly is: a being of light and love. When I saw her as only that, my vision of what was happening in the physical shifted. I was experiencing what we call a miracle in the course's terminology: a shift in perception. When I looked past the noise, the words, the problem, I just saw my mom's face, and I saw her as she truly was. In that moment, all the yelling dropped away and peace revealed itself to me in the present moment.

It is a moment I will never forget.

From that experience, I knew in my heart that peace does not come from seeking answers to external problems. Instead, peace comes from turning within to discover what was never lost.

The world is seeking peace, but it is not something that can be sought and found. We will not discover peace by fighting each other, and it certainly will not come by killing each other. These are truly insane ways of trying to create peace. What we need to learn is that peace is not acquired, and it is never lost. Peace exists everywhere, all around us, in every moment. Peace is.

Peace is not waiting for some victory on a distant shore.
Peace is waiting on everyone's doorstep.
Peace is waiting to be invited in – to be fully desired.
And when you invite peace into your life, it simply uncovers itself and reveals all its glory.

INVITING PEACE IN

I had a very clear vision of this reality one day as I was sitting in meditation. In this vision, I saw myself in a house other than my own, having tea with three beautiful beings called Peace, Joy, and Love. I did not know how I knew this, but I knew exactly who was sitting on the couch across from me.

We were having a lovely conversation, laughing and joking, when the doorbell rang loud and clear. I got up from my seat and opened the door to find three more beings called Conflict, Anger, and Attack. They demanded to be let in.

"Why have I not been invited in?" Anger asked as he pushed me aside.

I just stood there with my mouth open, completely taken aback. The trio did not care. They rushed past me and demanded to be served some tea. I noticed Love got up off the couch and poured a cup of tea for Anger before quietly slipping away. Joy and Peace followed Love's lead, serving Conflict and Attack with beverages and offering them places on the couch.

Before long, I was in a heated debate with Anger about who owned this house. Anger seemed to think the whole place belonged to him, but Conflict was absolutely certain it was her place, and she wasn't being pushed out by anyone. The debate raged on with great speed, going back and forth like a tennis ball being batted across the room. In quite a short period of time, I grew bored with all the fighting and chaos and drifted up and over to the living room window.

Where had Love, Joy, and Peace gone? I wondered.

I looked outside and saw the three of them sitting on a bench in the garden and enjoying the sunshine. Suddenly, I realized what I had done. I turned around and walked to the door, opened it, and then firmly asked Anger, Conflict, and Attack to leave my house right now. They looked up, confused, and then immediately started to argue and attack each other.

In a loud voice, I told them, "I mean it. Please leave, now."

With disbelief written all over their faces, they slowly rose up, looked all around as if there was some mysterious force lurking behind a table or chair, and started for the open door. I could hear them commenting under their breath.

"Well, I have never been treated so rudely," said Anger.

"Who is to blame for this outrageous behaviour?" said Conflict.

"Can you believe it? Kicking me out! Of all the nerve!" said Attack.

I laughed as they stumbled down the stairs, still arguing, attacking, and creating conflict between each other. As I stood outside on the porch in the warm sunshine, I called out to Joy, Love, and Peace to come on back and finish their tea. I missed them and wanted to return my home to the happy state it in been in before such a rude interruption. And that's exactly what happened. The trio got up from the bench and returned, smiling and peaceful, to resume drinking tea with me.

When my meditation ended, I laughed to myself. How silly, but how significant. Isn't this just what we all do, every day? Joy, Love and Peace are happy to be our companions, but instead we answer the call of Anger, Conflict, Attack, and whatever other shady creatures come knocking at our door, including:

- Frustration
- Greed
- Blame
- Resentment
- Fear
- Envy
- Jealousy
- Rage
- Sadness
- Depression

It's insane, really! I acknowledged to myself.

Who comes knocking on your door?

Instead of inviting these strangers in to live with you, take a moment and pause. Instead of answering their call, why not send them packing? Or, the next time they come knocking just do not answer the door!

WHAT DOES *A COURSE IN MIRACLES* SAY ABOUT PEACE?

Everyone wants peace, but it is certainly not something we find easily in the physical world. Our physical world is a world of duality – a world where everyone has their own interpretation of events. Conflicts, pain, war, and suffering come from seeing the world differently and insisting we are each right. However, there is a famous line from *A Course in Miracles* that says, "Would you rather be right or happy?" We must decide that we value peace more than being right.

Peace is not found, it is revealed. It is something we choose in our minds, and then it is revealed to us because it is already there. Here is how *A Course in Miracles* puts it:

> *The Thought of peace was given to God's Son*
> *the instant that his mind had thought of war.*
> *There was no need for such a Thought before,*
> *for peace was given without opposite, and merely was.*
> *But when the mind is split there is a need of healing.*
> *So, the Thought that has the power to heal the split*
> *became a part of every fragment of the mind*
> *that still was one but failed to recognize its oneness.*
> *Now it did not know itself, and thought its own Identity was lost.*
>
> *Salvation is undoing in the sense that it does nothing,*
> *failing to support the world of dreams and malice.*
> *Thus, it lets illusions go. By not supporting them,*
> *it merely lets them quietly go down to dust. And what they hid is now revealed;*
> *an altar to the holy Name of God whereon His Word is written,*
> *with the gifts of your forgiveness laid before it,*
> *and the memory of God not far behind.*
> W, L230, 2:2-3

PEACE IS THE NATURAL INHERITANCE OF SPIRIT

"Peace is the natural inheritance of spirit. Everyone is free to refuse to accept his inheritance, but he is not free to establish what his inheritance is. The problem everyone must decide is the fundamental question of authorship."
T, 3, VI, 10:1-3

PEACE IS THE STATE WHERE LOVE ABIDES

"Peace is the state where love abides, and seeks to share itself. Conflict and peace are opposites."

T, 23, I, 12:5

PEACE COMES FROM COMPLETE FORGIVENESS

"You who want peace can find it only by complete forgiveness."

T, 1, VI, 1:1

PEACE IS THE EGO'S ENEMY

"Peace is the ego's greatest enemy because, according to its interpretation of reality, war is the guarantee of survival."

T, 5, III, 5:5

IF YOU WANT PEACE, YOU MUST GIVE UP THE IDEA OF CONFLICT ENTIRELY

"The truth is total, the untrue cannot exist. Commitment to either must be total; they cannot coexist in your mind without splitting it. If they cannot coexist in peace, and if you want peace, you must give up the idea of conflict entirely and for all time."

T, 7, VI, 8:8-9

WHEN PEACE IS NOT WITH YOU ENTIRELY

"Only this is certain in this shifting world that has no meaning in reality: When peace is not with you entirely, and when you suffer pain of any kind, you have beheld some sin within your brother, and have rejoiced at what you thought was there. Your specialness seemed safe because of it."

T, 24, IV, 5:2-3

GOD PLACED PEACE IN YOUR HEART

"I place the peace of God in your heart and in your hands, to hold and share. The heart is pure to hold it, and the hands are strong to give it. We cannot lose."

T, 5, IV, 8:10-12

PART THREE

HAPPINESS:
An Ideal Life Versus an Authentic Life

*"Authenticity is a collection of choices
that we have to make every day.
It's about the choice to show up and be real.
The choice to be honest.
The choice to let our true selves be seen."*
Brené Brown, The Gifts of Imperfection

INTRODUCTION

HOW TO LIMIT PROBLEMS, CHAOS, AND DRAMA
Chaos

Truthfully, chaos is what we all experience here on the physical plane. There is disorder, pain, and confusion because we all believe different truths, and we all project those truths out onto the world. Then we defend our positions and fight over them in an insane effort to make ourselves feel safe and right. *A Course in Miracles* explains in detail how the laws of chaos really work. What follows is a quick summary of how we create chaos here on the physical, dualistic plane based on the teachings from *A Course in Miracles*.

First Chaotic Law: Truth Is Different for Everyone

The truth is different for everyone because everyone is separate and has their own thoughts that set them apart. This principle evolves from the belief there is a hierarchy of illusions; some are more valuable and therefore are true. Each person establishes this hierarchy for him/herself and makes it true by his/her attack on what other people value. This first law seems to establish degrees of truth among illusions.

What is really true, according to *A Course in Miracles?*

Truth is eternal – it is the same for everyone. There is no hierarchy in illusions; some are not more valuable than others. This is why *A Course in Miracles* states right at the beginning of the book:

> *"There is no order of difficulty in miracles.*
> *One is not 'harder' or 'bigger' than another.*
> *They are all the same. All expressions of love are maximal."*
>
> T, 1, I, 1:1-4

Second Chaotic Law: Everyone Is a Sinner

The second law of chaos is that everyone is a sinner and therefore deserves attack and death. This introduces the idea of fear. One person is stronger than another. One person has more than another. As a result, the Father and the Son now appear to be separated.

What is really true, according to *A Course in Miracles?*

There is no sin, just "mistakes or errors in perception" which can ultimately be corrected in the mind.

Third Chaotic Law: God Hates Us for What We Made

If God cannot be mistaken, He must accept His Son's belief in what he is and hate him for it. God must hate us for making a separate world where we hide from him.

What is really true, according to *A Course in Miracles?*

God does not accept or even know your belief in your self. God only knows who you are to him, and that never changes. To God, you are the Son of God, whole, perfect, and innocent. This is your natural inheritance, as you were created by the Father to be just like him. And God is eternal, pure love; if he acknowledged some our dreams of duality, he would not be eternal, pure love.

Fourth Chaotic Law: You Have What You Have Taken

The ego values only what it has taken from someone or something else. The belief behind this is that you have what you have taken, and that another's loss becomes your gain.

What is really true, according to *A Course in Miracles?*

You can never gain from someone else's loss. It is impossible to gain when a brother loses, because you are one with your brother. His loss is your loss; they are inseparable.

Fifth Chaotic Law: There Is a Substitute for Love

The final law of chaos holds that there is a substitute for love. This is the magic that will cure your pain, the missing factor in your madness that makes it "sane." This means that we think that something other than love can fix the problem. If only we talked enough, if only we got enough awards, if only we got what the neighbour had, if only we were skinny enough, if only we had more money... the list goes on and on. We believe there is a substitute for God's love, and we go about searching for it, striving for it, even dying for it.

What is really true, according to *A Course in Miracles?*

Only that which is eternal is true. Therefore, eternal love is true, and nothing else. We were created as extensions of God's eternal love. On this level, we have everything. By accepting God's love, we remember we have everything. Love is our eternal home. Love is all there is.

The Laws of Chaos Govern All Illusion.

If you follow the laws of chaos, you believe we are not one. You believe we are separate bodies, and that some thoughts are truer than other thoughts.

Our separation is strengthened by this belief through a hierarchy of illusions. For example, you feel that you must defend what you believe or it will be taken from you.

These laws of chaos govern all illusion. They set up all the conflict, strife, anger, hatred, and shadows the world offers.

HOW CAN THIS THOUGHT SYSTEM BE TRUE?

The laws of chaos make up an insane thought system. But who would cling to such madness? Here is what *A Course in Miracles* offers us on this subject:

> *"What protects madness is the belief that it is true.*
> *It is the function of insanity to take the place of truth.*
> *It must be seen as truth to be believed. And if it is the truth,*
> *then must its opposite, which was truth before, be madness now.*
> *Such a reversal, completely turned around, with madness sanity,*
> *illusions true, attack a kindness, hatred love and murder benediction,*
> *this the goals the laws of chaos serve.*
> *These are the means by which the laws of God appear to be reversed."*
>
> T, 23, II, 14:2-7

When we desire an ideal life, we typically want everything to go our way. We want everything beautiful and true to be here and now. Translated, that often means we want money, fame, success, a special partner, and more. But this is not an ideal life; this is life rooted in competition, changes, and degrees of success and failure.

Living an authentic life does not mean looking outside of yourself for success and happiness. It means looking within and discovering who you truly are.
- You are not your things.
- You are not your house, car, job, or accomplishments.
- You are not valued by the amount of money in your bank account.

At your very essence, you are an eternal spirit – whole, pure, and lacking in absolutely nothing. Let's look at a few ideas that will help us move closer to living an authentic life.

 # Chapter 11

PROBLEMS: Does the World Have Any Problems?

Western Thinking
- The world has many problems and many answers.

Reverse Thinking
- The world has one problem and one answer.

Chapter 11 – Problems:
Does the World Have Any Problems?
The world seems full of problems, and every night we tune in to see them on the news. Does this kind of thinking actually help? Find out what *A Course in Miracles* explains is the root of all problems.

bit.ly/problemsworld

THERE IS ONE PROBLEM AND ONE ANSWER:
MY PERSONAL EXPERIENCE WITH THIS REVERSE THOUGHT

One of my husband's and my favourite things to do is to get in the car and go on a road trip. The best part is that we do not plan where we will stay. Instead, we come up with a few guideposts for the holiday – a general outline of where we want to get to and when we want to get back – and then we jump in the car and go! It is adventure at its finest. During these kinds of driving holidays, we have discovered all sorts of places we never knew existed; after all, you can't plan to go to a place you do not know. Through this, we open our horizons and give ourselves a chance to be surprised and delighted.

One year, we were invited to a family wedding in Toronto. As we live in Vancouver on the west coast, we usually take a plane to visit that city because it is quite far away. But this time I wanted to see the country and go on a road trip. We decided to go down through the United States, up into Ontario, around Lake Superior, and then head to Toronto. We would stay with my husband's family for the weekend of the wedding and then head back home back across Canada.

A FORK IN OUR ROAD

Our holiday did not disappoint. On the first night, we found ourselves staying in the lovely little town of Grand Forks just north of the Canadian border. The next night, we just happened to be staying in the beautiful town of Bigfork, Montana. I thought this was odd – two nights, two forks. We certainly hadn't planned it that way, but now the trend was set. Throughout our holiday, we seemed to go from fork to fork, staying in Belle Fourche in South Dakota and The Forks in Winnipeg. It was so consistent that I wondered if the universe was trying to tell me something.
- Was I at a literal fork in the road of life?
- Was I being told through symbols to choose a new path?

I had certainly been thinking about the different areas of my life. I had my company, Creative Wonders Communications, for which I spent my days working as a Creative Director. In addition, I was spending a lot of time in the early mornings as a Director/Consultant for Business Networking International (BNI). Plus, I was holding *A Course in Miracles* study groups on Monday nights. To put the cherry on the cake, I was taking a ministry program to become a Reverend. I had a lot of questions.
- Should I retire because my husband had retired?
- Should I give up BNI?
- Should I close my business and just be a Reverend?

It did seem to me a little like I was at a possible metaphysical fork in the road.

- Did I need to give some things up?
- Did I need to close my business and just focus on *A Course in Miracles*?
- What was I to do?

Many people were telling me to just retire and enjoy life, but I was not ready to do that. REFIRE, maybe, but definitely not RETIRE. So, I was confused.

I decided to meditate. Yet every time I sat down, closed my eyes, and asked my D.I.G. (Divine Inner Guidance) why I was running into so many forks, I would not see a fork in the road. Instead, in my mind's eye, I saw a great big silver dinner fork. It did not make sense to me at first, but I am persistent, and eventually I got my answer.

My D.I.G. said, *You think you have to choose between the four prongs on the fork. You confuse yourself with so many choices. There really is one choice, and one choice only. It is not what you choose to do, it is how you choose to **handle it.***

Hearing that, I saw the handle of the fork highlighted in my vision. The voice continued. *We are not so concerned with what you are doing but with how you are doing it. In everything you do, you need to handle it the same way. You need to handle every situation in your life with great love. You need to eliminate judgment and fear. That is all. Handle everything with love.*

I laughed out loud. How confusing we make things for ourselves! We really think that one fork in the road is better than another, but what I learned from this visual meditation is simple: stop confusing the issue. It is my ego that is concerned about which **fork** to take; my soul knows that every fork leads to the same decision. Will I come from a place of fear, or will I come from a place of love?

Simply put, it is how I handle things that counts. I thought I had many problems, but now I could see there was one simple answer to all of them: whatever I did, I needed to do it with love. That is how to handle everything in life. Unfortunately, I do not always remember this simple lesson.

Here's another time when problems confused my mind.

WHAT TO DO IN THE MIDDLE OF THE NIGHT

For years, I have often woken up in the middle of the night. Some might say it is due to a hormone imbalance caused by menopause, but I always felt like I was being directed to turn my attention to my spiritual study. When you think about it, this is the perfect time to get up and read *A Course in Miracles* – my mind is rested and the house is quiet.

This came into play during an extremely busy time at work. I was writing five long marketing plans for **five different companies**, and each company had seemingly very different problems that I was addressing and attempting to solve. I was overwhelmed and feeling stuck.

When I woke up in the middle of the night during this tumultuous period at work, I did as I had so many nights before: I got up and went downstairs to study the course. I simply picked up the book, opened it to a random page, and started reading. As always, I was fascinated to discover that the passage I read was exactly applicable to what was going on inside of me.

When I opened the course this evening, I turned to Lesson 79 in the workbook, entitled:

Let Me Recognize the Problem So It Can Be Solved.

Wow, that caught my attention. I did feel like I had lots of problems, and I wanted the answers. I read on.

"The world seems to present you with a vast number of problems, each requiring a different answer."
W, L79, 4:2-5

"No one could solve all the problems the world appears to hold.
They seem to be on so many levels, in such varying forms
and with such varied content,
that they confront you with an impossible situation.
Dismay and depression are inevitable as you regard them.
Some spring up unexpectedly,
just as you think you have resolved the previous one.
Others remain unsolved under a cloud of denial,
and rise to haunt you from time to time,
only to be hidden again but still unsolved."
W, L79, 5:1-5

"All this complexity is but a desperate attempt not to recognize the problem,
and therefore not to let it be resolved."
W, L79, 6:1

What? Did the lesson say complexity hides the problem? This is an intriguing concept. I read on.

"If you could recognize that your only problem is separation,
no matter what form it takes, you could accept the answer
because you would see its relevance.
Perceiving the underlying constancy in all the problems that seem to confront you,
you would understand you have the means to solve them all."

W, L79, 6:2-3

And understand I did. After years and years of study, I did know what the course was speaking about. A literal light bulb went off inside my head, and a fantasy choir of angels sang in my ear.

For you to have the same light bulb moment I had that night, I will have to backtrack and fill in some blanks.

A BRIEF HISTORY OF HOW WE WENT FROM ONENESS AND LOVE TO SLEEPLESS NIGHTS AND ENDLESS STRUGGLES, ACCORDING TO *A COURSE IN MIRACLES*.

In the beginning, according to *A Course in Miracles*, there was just God – invisible, formless, timeless, eternal pure love. Do not think of him a person, but rather as an all-encompassing presence that is all-knowing, all-loving, and eternally beyond time and space, where no variation ever exists. In short, there is no change and no concept of duality with God. God simply is. Things get complex from here on out, so in the interest of keeping it simple I have spelled it out in numbered steps. Call it a step-by-step method of going from love and oneness to being up in the middle of the night worrying about a seemingly endless list of worldly problems.

Please note: this is a short summary of the myth of separation from God as told within *A Course in Miracles***.** It is the myth of separation, because in reality we are all safe at home in God forever. Unfortunately, we have forgotten this truth, and we now need to remember this by forgiving each other, ourselves, and the world. But I'm getting ahead of myself. Let's start at the beginning. It starts just like I said, with God.

1. God is formless and invisible. He is perfect, eternal love, light, and knowledge.

2. God extends his perfect, eternal love and light and creates "the one Son of God" (which is all of us). In this form, the Son of God is like the Father (invisible, light, love, and knowledge) but is NOT the Father. Sometimes this one Son is referred to as the one mind or the Christ mind.

3. Then, as the myth goes, one day the Son of God had a tiny, mad idea. I imagine it to be something like, "Could there be something else besides eternal love?" The course puts it this way:

> *"Into eternity, where all is one, there crept a tiny mad idea at which*
> *the Son of God remembered not to laugh.*
> *In his forgetting did the thought become a serious idea,*
> *and possible of both accomplishment and real effects."*
>
> T 27, VIII, 6:2-3

4. In order for a question or doubt to emerge in the one mind, there must be more than one thing. And for this to happen, the mind must split.

5. This split-in-mind births separation and consciousness: a right mind and a wrong mind. *A Course in Miracles* says:

> *"Consciousness, the level of perception,*
> *was the first split introduced into the mind after the separation,*
> *making the mind a perceiver rather than a creator.*
> *Consciousness is correctly identified as the domain of the ego.*
> *The ego is a wrong-minded attempt to perceive yourself as you wish to be,*
> *rather than as you are."*
>
> T 3, IV, 2:1-3

6. With consciousness, the Son-of-God has his first decision to make: he needs to decide what he wants to believe. In essence, he becomes **a decision maker**.

7. In this myth, the Son of God has now forgotten his home in God. So, he decides he must be **separate from God**, and in so doing, he denies heaven. In the course, this decision is called **the dream of separation.**

8. God answers this dream of separation with **the Holy Spirit**. The Holy Spirit's function is to be **the Voice for God** in our dream of separation.

9. The Holy Spirit is placed within the one mind forever to remind us of who we truly are and who our real Father is. In this way, the Holy Spirit speaks on behalf of God – he calls us home to God.

10. The Holy Spirit speaks for **right-mindedness**, or the state of mind that induces accurate perception. It is also called **miracle-mindedness** because it heals misperception and is the **Voice for Love**.

11. On the other hand, the ego speaks for **wrong-mindedness**. It is the questioning part of the mind that is the **Voice for Separation** or the **Voice for Fear**.

12. The ego, as the Voice for Fear, believes it must come up with elaborate strategies to keep the Son of God from choosing the Voice for Love and returning home to God. The ego believes this is the only way it can survive, and so it makes up complex strategies to achieve its goal.

13. **Ego Strategy #1:** Fearing God will be mad at us for separating from him, **guilt** is born in the ego. This is referred to as **The Secret Dream** of sin, guilt, and fear that demands punishment. (T, 27, VII, 2:4-7)

14. **Ego Strategy #2:** The ego is uncomfortable with The Secret Dream and wants to get rid of sin, guilt, and fear. So, the ego projects it out of the one mind. According to *A Course in Miracles*, the projection of the thought of separation creates the Big Bang and a physical universe emerges.

15. The Ego, as the spokesperson for fear, tells the One Son a story that goes something like this: "Now you have gone and done it! God will be mad at us. God will punish us. We need to hide, and the new physical universe looks like the perfect place to hide from God because we can be individuals. We can be separate, unique, and best of all, special."

16. The Son of God is lured by the ego's story of being special and so chooses the ego's thought system – the thought system of fear – over the thought system of love.

17. **Ego Strategy #3:** In order to be truly separate, bodies are created so the spirit can believe it is separate and special.

18. Now the Son of God is born into a body in the physical world and further forgets his true identity as spirit. The saving grace is that The Holy Spirit reminds us of our true heritage and continues to call us back home to God.

19. Meanwhile, back on Earth, we appear to be born into the physical world, not by our decision but by two parents – two other separated bodies.

20. Now we can claim we are not responsible for being here. It is our parent's fault. We did not ask to be born; we are innocent victims.

21. Now, as separate beings in separate families, we believe we have separate and special interests.

22. This belief creates competition, pain, anxiety, and confusion. We want out of the pain, so we search for love and meaning.

23. **Ego Strategy #4:** To answer our need for love and meaning, we make up **special loves** and **special hates.**

24. **Special loves** is the belief that there are special people that will fulfill our special needs. The ones who do not fulfill our needs can become our **special hates.**

25. We believe **we must acquire special loves and we must remove special hates. So, we attack our special hates** to protect ourselves and be safe.

26. But we are not safe. We look around and see people get sick, be hurt, and die.

27. This sickness and death proves we are right: we are not safe, and we must attack to stay safe.

28. Now we are in a hell of our own creation. Love is perceived as a threat to the ego.

29. We forget we are responsible for all the decisions we made along the way. With each step down the ladder from God, culminating in our physical bodies, we forget where we came from and our true origins.

30. Not remembering our true heritage as eternal love, we turn around and blame each other.

31. Now we believe it is the other person that must change.

32. Now we believe it is the world that needs to change.

RECOGNIZING THE PROBLEM

So, there I was, sitting up in the middle of the night, trying to solve all the problems in my own world. Suddenly, after reading Lesson 79 in the workbook, I saw that all my problems have this separation from God at their source. It became clear to me that no matter how complex my problems seem, every one of them can be traced back to our separation from God.

I suddenly felt strangely comforted. I thought, *No matter what my problems are, they can all be traced back to separation from God. Now I see that I am literally hiding in a confusion of my own making. All I need to do is let go of what I am thinking. I need to change my mind.*

The course elaborates on this point:

> *"We will try to free our minds of all the many different kinds of problems we think we have.*
> *We will try to realize that we have only one problem,*
> *which we have failed to recognize."*
> W, L79, 7:3-4

> *"Perhaps you will not succeed*
> *in letting all your preconceived notions go, but that is not necessary.*
> *All that is necessary is to entertain some doubt*
> *about the reality of your version of what your problems are."*
> W, L79, 8:2-3

I get it – these problems that are keeping me up at night are simply there because of how I am seeing my world. I am seeing complications. I am seeing problems.

I could see this situation differently. I could open my mind and realize the complications are just smoke screens designed to keep me away from the real truth about my origin. Now I could understand:

> *"Our efforts will be directed toward recognizing that*
> *there is only one problem and one answer.*
> *In this recognition are all problems resolved.*
> *In this recognition, there is peace."*
> W, L79, 9:3-5

In that state of recognition, I knew again that the world is full of complexity and confusion because I put it there. When I remembered that the one problem is separation from God, I remembered the one answer is to return to God. Return to love. Return to what is real and eternal. Our true nature is love – not special love, but eternal, holy love. That is what is unchanging; that is what is real. In this light, the physical world is an unreal complication of the mind.

In that moment, I told myself, Hold on to that thought. Find the peace that lives within. And with that thought, I returned to bed, earthly problems still complicated and unsolved but spiritual comfort returned. Thank you, Holy Spirit, Voice for God. I went back to sleep in heavenly peace.

WHAT DOES *A COURSE IN MIRACLES* SAY ABOUT PROBLEMS?

A Course in Miracles says one of the ego's greatest tactics is to give us problems – the more complex the problems, the better. That way, trying to sort them out takes us time, lots of time. It distracts us from our inner spirit and puts our focus squarely on the physical world. We become confused, frustrated, depressed, and anxious. In this scenario, the ego is clearly winning. It is at times like this that we need to turn inward.

> *"Inward is sanity; insanity is outside of you.*
> *You believe it is the other way; that truth is outside,*
> *and error and guilt within. Your little, senseless substitutions,*
> *touched with insanity and swirling lightly off on a mad course*
> *like feathers dancing insanely in the wind, have no substance.*
> *They fuse and merge and separate, in shifting and totally meaningless patterns*
> *that need not be judged at all. To judge them individually is pointless.*
> *Their tiny differences in form are no real differences at all.*
> *None of them matters.*
> *That they have in common and nothing else."*
>
> T, 18, I, 7:4-11

We frustrate ourselves further when we think we have to solve our problems all by ourselves. Yet within each of us is the power and love of God; it was built right into you at your creation. Instead of trying to solve complex problems outside of ourselves, we will be better equipped to deal with the outer if we first learn to align with the power within. This power knows not only what is best for us, but also what is best for all concerned.

How can we ever know what is best for everyone? It is just too much pressure. Instead, take your problems inside, hand them over to the Holy Spirit, and then step back and watch the miracles emerge. It is a fascinating and awe-inspiring process.

The application of the course, not the theory, is what changes and delights me. The theory is often difficult and hard to accept, and for years my ego argued with the ideas or just plain did not understand them. But when we let go and trust God, we open the door to the miraculous. As the course says:

> *"The mind returns to its proper function only when it wills to know.*
> *This places it in the service of spirit, where perception is changed."*
>
> T, 3, IV, 5:6-7

YOU ASK THE QUESTION. THE ANSWER IS GIVEN.

"You merely ask the question. The answer is given. Seek not to answer, but merely to receive the answer as it is given. In preparation for the holy instant, do not attempt to make yourself holy to be ready to receive. That is but to confuse your role with God's. Atonement cannot come to those who think they must first atone, but only to those who offer it nothing more than simple willingness to make way for it."

T, 18, IV, 5:1-6

YOU THINK A THOUSAND CHOICES ARE CONFRONTING YOU

"You need to be reminded that you think a thousand choices are confronting you, when there is really only one to make. And even this but seems to be choice. Do not confuse yourself with all the doubts that a myriad of decisions would induce. You make but one. And when that one is made, you will perceive it was no choice at all. For truth is true, and nothing else is true."

W, L128, 4:1-6

LET ME RECOGNIZE THE PROBLEM SO IT CAN BE SOLVED

"Let me realize today that the problem is always some form of grievance that I would cherish. Let me also understand that the solution is always a miracle with which I let the grievance be replaced. Today I would remember the simplicity of salvation by reinforcing the lesson that there is one problem and one solution. The problem is the grievance; the solution is a miracle."

W, L90 (Reviews Lesson 79), 1-5

LET ME RECOGNIZE THAT MY PROBLEMS HAVE BEEN SOLVED

"I seem to have problems only because I am misusing time. I believe that problem comes first, and time must elapse before it can be worked out. I do not see the problem and the answer as simultaneous in their occurrence. That is because I do not yet realize that God has placed the answer together with the problem, so that they cannot be separated by time. The Holy Spirit will teach me this, if I will let Him. And I will understand it is impossible that I could have a problem which has not be resolved already."

W, L90 (Reviews Lesson 79), 3:1-7

# Chapter 12

SIGNIFICANCE: What Do I Believe About Myself?

Western Thinking
- I am insignificant.

Reverse Thinking
- I am magnificence.

Chapter 12 – Significance: What Do I Believe About Myself?
What creates significance? Is it the opinion of others? Is it academic degrees, or wealth, or life lessons? Watch this video to see what *A Course in Miracles* says about turning your insignificance into magnificence.

bit.ly/whatdobelieve

I AM MAGNIFICENCE:
MY PERSONAL EXPERIENCE WITH THIS REVERSE THOUGHT.

YOU ARE TOO BIG

All my life, people have told me, "You are too big!" They did not mean my weight or my height. They meant my presence.

One of my best friends used to say it to me all the time. It worried me. What did they mean, I am too big? I thought that maybe I needed to try to be smaller. What if I just dumb things down? Or perhaps I should try to not talk as much, or to shrink into the background. I really was not sure what to do, but clearly something had to change; what I was doing was getting bad reviews.

My mother used to say, "You are like Miss Piggy. Too demanding. Too sure of yourself. Too confident and pushy!"

She would also say, "You steamroll people with your opinions and your way of being. You need to shut up! Keep your opinions to yourself!"

All this feedback from my friends and family made me unsure of how to be in the world. It felt wrong to be me. Everyone had an opinion, and it was clear I could not keep everyone happy. My teachers at The Haven Institute called people who depended on the opinions of others more than they depended on their own "field dependent." I did not like that label, but I had to admit that I had trained myself to be small, to hide my talents, and to not talk about myself too much.

My mother would say, "If anyone wants to know something about you, they will ask. Otherwise, it is rude to talk about yourself."

The message from the world seemed to be:
- Stay small.
- Stay under the wire.
- Don't stand out.
- Don't speak up.

Then, *A Course in Miracles* taught me something that was shocking at first. For me, it was truly a reversal in thinking:
"Be not content with littleness.
But be sure you understand what littleness is, and why you could never be content with it.
Littleness is the offering you give yourself.
You offer this in place of magnitude, and you accept it."

T, 15, III, 1:1-4

"Every decision you make stems from what you think you are,
and represents the value that you put upon yourself.
Believe the little can content you,
and by limiting yourself you will not be satisfied.
For your function is not little, and it is only by finding your function
and fulfilling it that you can escape from littleness."

T, 15, III, 3:3-5

In general, I have found that the world does not empower people. Instead, the world wants you to know your place. It suggests that one person is insignificant in the big scheme of things. Think of the size of the universe. What can one person do?

I can think of many people who taught me this lesson. For example, a client once said to me, "We are all as important as a hand in a bucket of water. Remove the hand, and you are instantly replaced." Ouch! That seemed harsh.

Here's another real-life story.

A while back, I had been acting as the Creative Director of the creative department in a large advertising agency for almost a year. One day, I got up the courage to go and ask for the official title and salary to go along with the job that I was already performing.

I was told by my superior, "You cannot be the Creative Director. You are going to leave and have babies soon."

I could not believe what I was hearing. I thought to myself, What about all the male Creative Directors who had been hired and swiftly fired one after another in the last few years? Most of them never stayed in the agency for even a year. I had been at the agency for five years, and I was hardly leaving to have a baby tomorrow. Heck, I was not even married!

I was shocked, and I decided there and then that my days there were numbered. Obviously, they did not value my work. Perhaps they thought I was just putting in time until I could have children, but guess what? I never did have those children that my superior claimed I would most certainly have at any moment!

Today, I find the world is much more empowering place for women. There are many more female role models who are out there making a difference, from astronauts to writers. But I believe we have more work to do in this area. Beyond being role models, we need leaders who show us how to change our thinking.

According to *A Course in Miracles*, every single person is born from the magnificence of pure eternal love. To deny this internal wealth and believe instead that you are poor, unworthy, or small contradicts your natural-born inheritance. To quote *A Course in Miracles*:

> *"All your striving must be directed against littleness,*
> *for it does require vigilance to protect your magnitude in this world.*
> *To hold your magnitude in perfect awareness in a world of littleness is a task*
> *the little cannot undertake."*
>
> T, 15, III, 4:4-5

I want to stress that we need to flip this world's thought processes on their head. We need reverse thinking. You were born to shine. You were born from the magnificence of God, and when you deny this and try to content yourself with less than this, you are unhappy because you are not in alignment with the truth about who you authentically are.

Do not let the world tell you who you are.
- Search your soul.
- Search your heart.

You know deep inside yourself that you are far more than some insignificant speck within the universe. You have an important role to play. The world needs your love.

> *"Love is not little and love dwells in you, for you are host to Him.*
> *Before the greatness that lives in you, your poor appreciation*
> *of yourself and all the little offerings you give slip into nothingness."*
>
> T, 15, III, 8:6-7

> *"Holy child of God, when will you learn that only holiness can content you and give you peace?"*
>
> T, 15, III, 9:1

Today is the day to claim your rightful inheritance. You are a holy child of God. You are eternal love, and you have an eternal role to play.
- Find it!
- Find your function.
- Find your glory.

Shine your light, because all minds are joined in the one mind. And when you shine your light, it shines into the mind of everyone. How can that be small and insignificant?

WHAT DOES *A COURSE IN MIRACLES* SAY ABOUT MAGNIFICENCE?

I was taught that it is boastful to think too much of yourself – that it is egotistical (not to mention annoying) when others believe they are better than everyone else. I agree that when people believe they are better than others, they are separating themselves from the rest of us. This type of thinking definitely comes from the ego. However, when you join with spirit and recognize that everyone has access to the magnificence of the Holy Spirit, it is not ego that is speaking but rather the truth within. This truth does not separate us from each other, but instead sees that everyone has access to this magnificence.

What I know and believe in my heart is that we are more than we could ever imagine. We are more than we want to believe, and it is our power within that frightens us. That is why people said to me, "You are too big. Stay small."

It has taken me a long time to grow bold enough to honour the magnificence within. And yes, of course, I still lose it from time to time. But when I go back within myself and connect with "the all that is," I feel its power and its strength. It gives me courage to use my hands, my feet, and my eyes here in this world – to be part of what I truly am and live up to I was created to be. This truth is not reserved for one person; it is to be experienced by and extended to all. We are each a light, a flame, and our light can ignite the flame within others.

Do not stay small. Find your part in the Holy Spirit's plan and live it. Help release the world from littleness.
- Claim your power.
- Claim your magnificence.

BE NOT CONTENT WITH LITTLENESS

"Be not content with littleness. But be sure you understand what littleness is, and why you could never be content with it. Littleness is the offering you give yourself. You offer this in place of magnitude, and you accept it. Everything in this world is little because it is a world made out of littleness, in the strange belief that littleness can content you. When you strive for anything in this world in the belief that it will bring you peace, you are belittling yourself and blinding yourself to glory. Littleness and glory are the choices open to your striving and your vigilance. You will always choose one at the expense of the other."

T, 15, III, 1:1-8

EVERY DECISION YOU MAKE STEMS FROM WHAT YOU THINK YOU ARE

"Every decision you make stems from what you think you are, and represents the value that you put upon yourself. Believe the little can content you, and by limiting yourself you will not be satisfied. For your function is not little, and it is only by finding your function and fulfilling it that you can escape from littleness."

T, 15, III, 2:3-5

YOU DO NOT ASK TOO MUCH OF LIFE BUT FAR TOO LITTLE

"You do not ask too much of life, but far too little. When you let your mind be drawn to bodily concerns, to things you buy, to eminence as valued by the world, you ask for sorrow, not for happiness."

W, L133, 2:1-2

 # Chapter 13

HAPPINESS: Does Happiness Constantly Change?

Western Thinking
- Happiness changes.

Reverse Thinking
- Happiness is a constant.

Chapter 13 – Happiness: Does Happiness Constantly Change? What makes you happy? Does happiness seem to come and go in your life? Watch the video to find out why *A Course in Miracles* says happiness is a constant state.

bit.ly/happinesshappen

HAPPINESS IS A CONSTANT:
MY PERSONAL EXPERIENCE WITH THIS REVERSE THOUGHT

BEAUTY, TRUTH, AND LIBERTÉ

I had been a student of *A Course in Miracles* for many years, but I was often struggling to make sense of the text. In my reading and study group, the language of the course confused me.

For example, there is a chapter entitled, "I Need Do Nothing!" One of the people in my study group used this chapter to validate the idea that she did not need to do anything in the world. She proclaimed she was like an eastern monk, and that people should just support her.

I was astonished by this declaration, and my mind bombarded itself with inner questions.
- "Why was she the monk?
- Why did she deserve to be supported and not have to work?

Everyone else I knew was working hard to make a living. Why was she the exception?"

I felt her ego was using the course's words to justify her not wanting to work. However, I was not skilled enough at the time to really articulate why her interpretation did not ring true with me.

It has taken me some time to understand the truth behind the passage she was quoting. If you read the whole quote from *A Course in Miracles* it says:

> *"When peace comes at last to those who wrestle with temptation and fight*
> *against the giving in to sin;*
> *when the light comes at last into the mind given to contemplation,*
> *or when the goal is finally achieved by anyone, it always comes with just one happy realization;*
> *'I need do nothing.'"*
>
> T, 18, VII, 5:7

This passage is not talking about whether you should or should not work in the world. It is talking about how when peace comes at last to the mind, it comes with the realization that "I need do nothing." And that is because in the mind, peace has always been there. Peace is not found; peace is revealed.

In the early years of studying with my group, I found a lot of this type of "course confusion," especially when phrases were quoted in isolation. What really helped me was the discovery of Gary R. Renard's book, *The Disappearance of the Universe: Straight Talk About Illusions, Past Lives, Religion, Sex, Politics and the Miracles of Forgiveness.*

One of my oldest friends called me one day and said I had to read this new book on the course. I explained I was leaving for Italy the next day. "No problem," he explained, "I will come right over with the book for you to read on your trip." What a gift!

I started reading Gary's book on the flight over to Italy, and I was fascinated. Things that had long been debated in my study group were not only explained, but also clarified. It was done in a most interesting and offbeat manner, and my highlighter was going full-time all the way through the book.

It was the perfect book to take to the little town of Sommacolonia in Northern Tuscany, where my husband, a few friends, and I would live for a couple of weeks. Sommacolonia means "Colony on the Summit," and that is exactly what it was: a little medieval town on the top of a hill. No cars were allowed as the streets were made of cobblestone and far too narrow. No one spoke English, so this little mountaintop oasis was quiet to me. I could take my book and study under the grape arbour, and my thoughts would not be interrupted.

Being surrounded by a language I did not understand was such an interesting experience. I thought it would be isolating, but instead I found it freeing. I could truly concentrate and meditate deeply without being distracted by other people's conversations. And so, in the hills of Tuscany, I read Gary's book and thought deeply about the concepts in the course. It was a beautiful time for me.

The kitchen window boxes of the house we were staying in were planted with red geraniums. All my life, I had seen myself in a kitchen with red geraniums. Now here I was in that kitchen and it felt profoundly ordained – as if I knew this moment would come one day.

During this time, my husband and I were sleeping in an old metal bed with a photo of Jesus in an enamel oval in the headboard. I joked with my husband that I was sleeping with Jesus, but in many ways that was not far from the truth. I did feel like I was resting and learning in loving arms. I loved what I was learning and studying, but I found myself asking, Could love really be the answer? Can there really be a place where only love exists?

As if in answer to my questions, I woke suddenly from my restful slumber one night to find the most beautiful woman standing at the foot of my bed. She was taller than normal, almost up to the ceiling, and she was dressed in a beautiful flowing white gown with a blue silk ribbon tied around her bodice and waist. She had long flowing golden hair, and she was surrounded by light.

She said, "I am Beauty, Truth, and Liberté."

I remember it distinctly because she did not say liberty, like I would say it in English. She said liberté, which I knew was French.

I did not understand what I was seeing. Was she a vision? An angel? A waking dream? A hallucination?

I did not have too much time to wonder, though, because she told me she was here to show me something. She asked me to close my eyes and journey with her to a place of only love. So, I closed my eyes, and together we seemed to journey beyond the earth, beyond the galaxies, to a place where all I could feel was a deep, unending, eternal love.

Telepathically, she told me, "There is a place where only love exists. In fact, it is all there is – eternally – and this place is available to all."

I started to sob within my vision. I could not believe it, but I could feel it: a place of eternal love and happiness.

This place felt like nothing I had ever experienced on earth, and it felt like a miracle to me. I sobbed with pure joy even though I did not have a body in this place. I did not have the physical eyes to cry, or to see the beautiful being I appeared to be travelling with.

I sobbed harder. My heart was breaking – breaking open to the possibility I wanted more than anything else. I wanted to know that love and only love truly exists, and here was my answer. Together, we both disappeared into the light and love.

I fell back asleep.

In the morning, I felt I had truly been visited by a being of light, and that I now knew something I had doubted before. Now, I was certain, love and happiness are not variables.

- Love is.
- Happiness is.
- Love IS the answer.

This real love – eternal love – is not the special love we often identify with here on earth. It is something beyond the physical, beyond the emotional, literally beyond ordinary comprehension, and it exists eternally and without change. And with this experience, I had felt it and proved it to myself.

WHAT DOES *A COURSE IN MIRACLES* SAY ABOUT HAPPINESS?

Who doesn't want happiness? Everyone wants to live a happier life; it is a universal desire and a calling of the heart.

The happiness we experience here on earth is fleeting – it shifts and changes, often from moment to moment. In Italy, I wanted to know that only love, eternal love, is true, and my vision helped me accept this inner reality. It seemed impossible to me in the physical world because this world is all about change. According to the course, though, there is another world where things do not change and alter.

 I found this concept hard to accept – it was so foreign to me here on Earth – until I was shown unchanging, eternal love and happiness by Beauty, Truth, and Liberté. It was overwhelming and unforgettable, just like my near-death-experience. It was in a realm beyond my wildest dreams, and yet miraculously, I experienced it.

As I have worked with the course over many decades, I have discovered that this realm is not a dream – it is a reality that lies within each of us. However, it takes some work and purification to experience this reality.

A Course in Miracles can show us the way. It clearly states it cannot teach love, for that is beyond what can be taught. Instead, it can help us remove the blocks to the awareness of love's presence within. And this eternal love has many attributes, including light, knowledge, and true happiness.

THE CONSTANCY OF HAPPINESS
"The constancy of happiness has no exceptions; no change of any kind. It is unshakable as is the Love of God for his creations."
T, 21, VIII, 2:3-4

THE GOOD, THE BEAUTIFUL AND THE HOLY
"Child of God you were created to create the good, the beautiful and the holy."
T, 1, VII, 2:1

HAPPINESS IS ATTAINED BY GIVING UP THE WISH FOR THE INCONSTANT
"Elusive happiness, or happiness in changing form that shifts with time and place, is an illusion that has no meaning. Happiness must be constant, because it is attained by giving up the wish for the inconstant."
T, 21, VII, 13:1-2

IF YOU SEE HAPPINESS AS EVER CHANGING

"No one decides against his happiness, but he may do so if he does not see he does it. And if he sees his happiness as ever changing, now this, now that, and now an elusive shadow attached to nothing, he does decide against it."

T, 21, VII, 12:5-6

HAPPY DREAMS

"Happy dreams come true, not because they are dreams, but only because they are happy. And so, they must be loving. Their message is, 'Thy Will be done,' and not, 'I want it otherwise.'"

T, 18, V, 4:1-3

 # Chapter 14

LUCK: Is It Luck to Be in the Right Place at the Right Time?

Western Thinking

- Being in the right place at the right time is luck.

Reverse Thinking

- You are always in the right place at the right time.

Chapter 14 – Luck: Is It Luck to Be in the Right Place at the Right Time?
Do you believe in luck? Do you believe you are never lucky? Watch this video to find out what *A Course in Miracles* teaches about luck and the reverse way of thinking about it.

bit.ly/luckisit

YOU ARE ALWAYS IN THE RIGHT PLACE AT THE RIGHT TIME: MY PERSONAL EXPERIENCE WITH THIS REVERSE THOUGHT.

THE ROAD LESS TRAVELLED

From early on in my life, I knew I was going to have twins. For years I spoke with a boy and a girl in my dreams who said they were my children, and that they would be coming to see me soon. I was confident of this fact, although I rarely discussed what I knew with anyone except my sisters.

In my early thirties, I was in a relationship with a man who wanted to get married. He was and still is an amazing person, but I was conflicted and wanted to answer some deep internal questions for my own inner peace before moving forward.

My parents, family, and friends all wanted me to marry this man, and I was torn between my inner longing and my need to make people happy and do the right thing. I felt an external pressure to be like everyone else – to get married and have a family. It seemed like the next logical step at the time, but I was not feeling happy about it.

I knew I needed to work on myself, and I felt becoming a mother and a wife would delay that work because I would spend my time being focused on others. I wanted the time and space to explore my inner questions, but the pressure was on.

My boyfriend eventually gave me a ring and asked me to marry him. It was awful. I wanted to make him happy, to make my parents happy, and to have a family, but something deep inside was calling me to follow another path.

I stayed up every night for about a week, roaming the house, looking up at the stars, and asking myself what I was going to do.

It seemed everybody loved my boyfriend. Even my best friend said she would slap me across the face if I did not marry this man.

What is wrong with you? I thought to myself.

I did not seem to want what everyone else wanted. I did not want to get married just for the sake of getting married, or because everyone else was doing it. I wanted to feel like it was the right thing to do.

I was conflicted. I was in pain. I was confused. I was plain unhappy. Eventually, I decided I had to listen to my inner self and not get married. Instead of finding a partner, I needed to find myself. And so, I broke off the engagement and broke the heart of my boyfriend, parents, friends, and family.

My boyfriend and I had been living together, so next came the painful task of moving out and watching the hurt on everyone's face. I felt terrible.

Then, I had a dream in which I told the twins I had decided not to get married. They were so angry. They told me I had a contract with them and could not just change my mind like that. I told them *I was sorry, but I had to listen to my heart.*

I never saw the twins in my dreams again. It looked like they were gone for good, angry about my decision. In fact, it appeared everyone was disappointed in me – both in the real world and in my dream world. Heck, even I felt disappointed with myself.

What was I doing?

I really could not answer the question. It felt awful, but it did feel aligned with something deep within me. So, I went blindly forward.

One truly lovely thing did happen during that time: I received a bouquet of flowers from a girlfriend who lived far away in California. When I opened the card, I almost collapsed on the ground with grief and relief. It said, "Congratulations for taking the road less travelled."

Reading this just made me break down and weep. Somebody finally understood. I could go on.

I knew that deciding not to get married in my early thirties might mean I would not have a family, and this made me sad. On some level, I felt like I was choosing between having a family and having myself. However, I did not want to pass along the pain and loneliness I felt to the next generation; I wanted to understand it and heal it before I raised children. So, with that in mind, I took the risk. I went off and did all my inner exploration and developed my inner world.

FAST FORWARD

As it turns out, I did not have children of my own; however, I do have stepchildren. Years later, when I was forty, I married a man who had two grown daughters. It was not my perfect vision, but it was my perfect choice.

By the time I got married, I knew who I was, and I knew I was not marrying my husband just so he could fulfill me. I felt whole in a way I had not felt in my early thirties, and I knew I was in charge of my happiness.

It was not his job to make me happy – that job lay squarely in my court and in my mind. I knew we were two adults getting married who did not need each other, but who wanted to be together and support each other as a team. It was a good feeling.

We talked about having children. He had raised his daughters on his own for the last decade, and he said he loved the idea of raising kids in a true partnership. I loved the idea too. Unfortunately, that's not what happened. We could not reverse his vasectomy, which meant we would have to go the route of fertility treatments. He lost interest, and I did not want to have children without a fully committed partner. I did not want him to turn to me years later when the children were misbehaving and hear the words, "Well, they are your kids, not mine!" My heart felt sad, but I clearly knew I had made the right choice. I did not feel like a victim on any level.

THE NEXT CHAPTER

Right at the time my husband and I announced our engagement, my two sisters announced they were both pregnant. I wanted them to be in our wedding party, and they asked if we could wait to get married until after the babies were born and they had stopped breastfeeding. As my husband and I were living together, it did not matter to us if we got married quickly. So, we waited almost two years to tie the knot.

One day, after I was long married, I went to a psychic who said to me, "You have two children."

I said, "I have two stepchildren."

"No," she said, "You have two children."

I told her she must be mistaken, but she insisted. "The children did not come to you; they came to your two sisters. They are twins, and they wanted to come as close together as they could. So, they came one to each of your sisters."

I was astonished! I had always felt close to my sister's eldest children – the ones I had held off my wedding for. In fact, it had crossed my mind many times that they were the twins from my dreams, but I had not dared to pursue that line of thought. Now, however, I was being confronted with it.

In my heart of hearts, I knew it was true. I wondered if I should discuss this with my sisters, but I did not want to hurt them in any way. What would they think? I decided it probably wasn't a good idea to talk to them, so I kept quiet.

It took many, many years before I found the moment when I finally told my sisters what the psychic had told me. When I did, they both looked at each other with shock on their faces.

"Oh no!" I said, "Now I have really done it."

"We never wanted you to know!" they both told me.

"What do you mean?" I replied.

"We always knew they were the twins you had spoken of years ago, but we thought you would be sad if you knew they came to us."

"What?" I exclaimed. "I clearly made that decision, and I am not sad in any way. I thought you might be sad."

We laughed and hugged. The children of my dreams were with us. I felt so happy and so relieved. My sisters said they were happy I knew. It felt like a true revelation. In my heart, I suddenly knew that the people who are meant to be with you, will be with you.

There are no accidents. Love always finds a way.
There is only divine timing, which is always now.

Although I had taken the road less travelled, I realized I cannot take a wrong turn.

WHAT DOES *A COURSE IN MIRACLES* SAY ABOUT LUCK?

According to *A Course in Miracles*, there is no such thing as luck. Luck is a man-made concept created by wrong-mindedness or fearful thoughts. Luck means people can be singled out and separated from one another – some are lucky, some are not.

The course tells us that one person is not lucky and the other a victim of chance or timing. Instead, the physical universe operates under strict rules of cause and effect. The cause is the one mind and, more specifically, the ideas or thoughts held in our one shared mind. The world is the product of these thoughts, which are projected out of this mind like a giant hologram. To put it another way, for something to exist in the hologram, it first must exist in the one mind. This means there is design and intent behind everything. We do not see it because we do not want to see it. We repress thoughts of wholeness and equality under thoughts of the ego that believes in separation, sin, and guilt.

The ego wants us to believe in chance or luck because then we do not have to be responsible for what we see in our world. We can cast blame out onto other people, the environment, our food, our parents, and of course, our government. When we believe we do not have control, we can believe in the luck of the draw. However, the course points out that the exact opposite is true. We are responsible for what we see, but many minds have repressed and forgotten this because it makes us feel uncomfortable – it makes us feel guilty. And that is something we do not want.

A Course in Miracles clearly teaches that we are responsible for what we see in our world. We made it through our thoughts, which means we can change it through our thoughts. But as we share the one mind, we cannot do this alone; we need each and every person to fulfill their role.

How can we do this? The course says we must look at everything around us and realize we could change what we see. Instead of seeing a world where we have no power, we can take back our power and see things differently. The world does not need to imprison us; in fact, the world can free us if we decide to see everyone for who they truly are and not their behaviour. Look at what you do not like – the judgments, the criticism – and see what exists beyond the masks of the physical.

Everyone is connected to the Holy Spirit, and if she cannot see her true identity, we can see it and hold it for her. We can unchain ourselves and our brothers and sisters when we acknowledge there is more to each and every one of us than our eyes can see. Every person and every situation can be an opportunity, a doorway to step through to the truth. Rather than the world enslaving you, it can free you. You do not need luck; you need to awaken the truth that lies within.

YOUR PASSAGE THROUGH TIME AND SPACE IS NOT RANDOM

"Your passage through time and space is not random. You cannot but be in the right place at the right time. Such is the strength of God. Such are His gifts."

W, L42, 2:3-5

THERE IS ANOTHER WAY OF LOOKING AT THE WORLD

"Since the purpose of the world is not the one I ascribed to it, there must be another way of looking at it. I see everything upside down, and my thoughts are the opposite of truth. I see the world as a prison for God's Son. It must be, then, that the world is really a place where he can be set free. I would look upon the world as it is, and see it as a place where the Son of God finds his freedom."

W, L57, 3 (33):2-6

WHEN I SEE THE WORLD AS A PLACE OF FREEDOM

"When I see the world as a place of freedom, I realize that it reflects the laws of God instead of the rules I made up for it to obey. I will understand that peace, not war, abides in it. And I will perceive that peace also abides in the hearts of all who share this place with me."

W, L57, 4 (34):2-4

EVERY IDEA BEGINS IN THE MIND OF THE THINKER

"As we have already emphasized, every idea begins in the mind of the thinker. Therefore, what extends from the mind is still in it, and from what it extends it knows itself. The word 'know' is correct here, because the Holy Spirit still holds knowledge safe in your mind through His impartial perception. By attacking nothing, He presents no barrier to the communication of God. Therefore, being is never threatened. Your Godlike mind can never be defiled. The ego never was and never will be part of it, but through the ego you can hear and teach and learn what is not true. You have taught yourself to believe that you are not what you are."

T 6, III, 1:1-8

Chapter 15

CHANGE: What Do I Need to Change?

Western Thinking
- I need to change the world.

Reverse Thinking
- I need to change my thinking about the world.

Chapter 15 – Change: What Do I Need to Change?
Have you ever wanted someone in your life to change? Watch this video to learn what *A Course in Miracles* teaches us to do when we want to change others.

bit.ly/whatdoichange

I NEED TO CHANGE MY THINKING ABOUT THE WORLD:
MY PERSONAL EXPERIENCE WITH THIS REVERSE THOUGHT

After my father died, my sister started to see pennies everywhere she went. She told me that whenever she saw a penny, she thought it was a message from Dad. I liked the idea, so I started to look for my own pennies from heaven. And once I did, I started to find them everywhere – even where I least expected them. Here is a story that wonderfully illustrates how pennies from heaven changed my world view.

MESSAGES FROM THE ETERNAL

Just after my dad died, a woman named Penny emailed me. She had seen my dad's obituary in the local newspaper and wondered if I was the Diane Lund that used to be in her ballet school. I was shocked; I had not heard from Penny in over thirty years. I had started to take ballet lessons from her at the age of five and continued to dance with her until she had asked another student, Sue, and I to take over her ballet school so she could focus on becoming a schoolteacher. She asked, "Would you like to get together and catch up?"

As I was grieving and trying to deal with my mother, who had developed fibromyalgia right after my dad died, I asked if we could meet in a few months. She agreed and said she would try and find Sue to join us. I thought it was a wonderful idea to have this reunion.

The months flew by, and soon we were all gathered together to have lunch at a local restaurant. It was a homecoming for sure. Penny brought an album packed with photos of Sue and I in her many dance recitals. There were pictures of us dressed as Russian dancers, as soldiers, as cowgirls, and as ballerinas of course, in various coloured tutus with tiaras in our tightly up-done hair. It was a trip down memory lane.

At one point, Penny turned to me and said, "Diane there are no more photos of you unfortunately. Your mom asked me to stop giving you lead roles or putting you in the front. She did not want photos taken of you, or for you to be treated in any special way. She was worried it might go to your head."

"Well, that explains a lot!" I said. "I always wondered why I stopped getting lead roles. I thought maybe I just was not as good as Sue."

"No," said Penny, "you were an amazing child and a good dancer."

I wondered, *Why did my mom want to hide me? Why did she want me NOT to excel?* It was an ongoing question in my life. My mother had always wanted to hide my talents and gifts. As I wrote in Book I, I would come home with a great report card – all A's and B's – and my mom would look at it and tuck it in a drawer under the dishtowels. Then she would take my sister's report card that was all C's and tape it to the fridge. She would tell me that I needed to make a fuss over my sister and her grades. I was left wondering, *Why was no one making a fuss over me? Why did I need to be silenced?*

The next time I saw my mother after the reunion, I asked her, "Why did you ask Penny to put me in the back row and not treat me special?"

My mom was outraged. "Penny just made all that up! I never said anything remotely like that to her."

I was not buying my mom's version of the story. Why would Penny say such a thing if it were not true? There was nothing for her to gain from it.

Once again, my childhood confusion reigned in my brain. As I sat there, Penny's words – that I was an amazing child – rang in my ears. Then, I heard my father's voice speaking deep inside of my being. *Penny speaks the truth, Diane. I am sorry we kept this knowledge to ourselves. I am sorry we wanted to hide you away.*

Wow, I thought. It felt like Penny was giving voice to the words my dad wanted me to hear. *Is my dad using this "Penny" to tell me what he wanted me to know from the other side?*

Pay attention to Penny, the voice within urged. I was shocked that spirit was working in such miraculous ways. In the days that followed, I became convinced that my dad was using Penny's earthly voice as his heavenly voice. I must admit, I found it healing to hear the truth.

PAY BACK TIME

A couple of months later, Penny was having a big birthday party and wanted Sue and me to attend. Unfortunately, Sue could not make it. I did not want to go alone, but Penny really seemed to want me to come. So, I gathered my courage and drove to Penny's friend's place for her birthday celebration.

As soon as I was in the house, I knew that going had been the right thing to do. Penny was ecstatic to see me. She hugged me tightly and rushed me up the stairs to introduce me to her friends. A little while later, a bell rang and Penny started to give a speech. I could not believe her words. She thanked everyone for coming, and then started to say that she wanted to introduce everyone to me. She said the reason everyone was in this room was because of me.

I was shocked. "Because of me?" I could hardly believe my ears.

Penny continued, "Diane was one of my earliest ballet students, and she made me realize how much I love teaching. Because of her, I went into teaching and met everyone in this room!"

It was an honour to hear this. Imagine that thirty years later, someone lets you know how your life changed theirs. You just never know how you affect people.

I was really touched, but I could not let this compliment go by without delivering my own miraculous change in thinking to Penny.

I told the crowd how I met Penny when I was five and took ballet lessons from her for over a decade, but then I did not see her again for thirty years. I explained how my dad seemed to be communicating with my sisters and I through the manifestation of pennies. We were finding physical pennies everywhere. In fact, on one occasion my husband and I found a literal piggy bank full of pennies dumped at our mailbox. How on the earth did that happen? To this day, we have no idea where all those pennies came from.

But my dad did not stop there. He brought the real Penny back into my world. Penny reached out and told me the truth about parts of my childhood that had always felt like big, unexplained holes. Now I understood what had happened in my past – both the good and the bad – and that knowing was deeply healing. I felt peace, and this peace changed my thinking about my world. I could forgive my mom and dad for doing what they thought was right for me. I understood my ideas about not being good enough way back when were not true. I was able to change my thinking, and this changed my world.

CHANGE IS THE CONDITION OF THE SEPARATED WORLD

Change is the condition of the separated world. It lives and dies, literally, on the belief in change.

My mother used to say, "We all live and we all die; that is the one thing we all will do." She spoke of the inevitability of the physical world, where all things appear to have their time and then disappear. Deep down, that is why we don't like change: we fear the end of things. We fear losing things, especially things we love. We are not secure in the idea that we are eternal – that love is eternal – because change in the physical world seems to prove otherwise.

A Course in Miracles addresses our confusion. It says we have to look past the visible to the invisible realms. We think that what we cannot see with our physical eyes is not occurring, when in reality we know this is not true.

What is invisible can touch us – like how the wind can blow our hair or toss the clouds around. Invisible airwaves can send out songs that can be picked up by a radio and delivered to us at the precise moment we may need inspiration.

The invisible can free us if we are willing to look beyond the physical, which is only a thin veil over the eternal that lives within everyone and everything.

In my life, the veil between the physical world and the invisible world was lifted by my belief that there is no death, and that we can communicate with everyone – even those who are gone from this plane. Penny is one of the many instruments the universe has used to help me understand there is so much more to us and to the world than what we can see with our naked eyes.

The western world is hyper focused on the physical world as if it is the be-all-to-end-all of life. We have a cult of admiring the rich and famous, and if we hold this measuring stick up to ourselves, we will almost always come up short. There will always be people who are better off than we are, people who are richer, prettier, better at sports, happier, having more sex, travelling more, just fill in the blank.

A Course in Miracles takes the opposite viewpoint. Most of who you are in the physical world has been made up – it is your ego self, the self that is full of desires, judgments, and expectations. If you trust, put what you think you want out there in the world, and then go on and push for it, you may just get it. However, life often delivers some heavy, disappointing, and frustrating blows to your plans.

Why?

It is the nature of the physical world to be ever changing. The job that was perfect yesterday is not perfect today. The person who said they loved you wants a divorce. The economy that was robust has gone bust. And so the world turns.

So, what is the way out?

SEEK TO CHANGE YOUR MIND, NOT THE WORLD.
You must change your mind in order to change the world you see.

If you need something from the world, you have once again given your power to something that is out of your control – something that is beyond you. However, once you no longer need anything from the world for yourself because you have found what you need in the inner, you are now free to live a truly amazing life.

Rather than trusting in your own power, trust in the power within.

You don't know everything there is to know about every situation; however, there is someone who does know. Trust the voice of the Holy Spirit within to give you the answers. Trust your inner D.I.G. (Divine Inner Guidance).

What you need is not on the outside. It cannot be found in a job, in your children, in winning a game, or in becoming rich. Trust that you need only one thing: you need to be tuned into your inner spirit so you can access the power of the universe rather than your own limited power.

Once you approach life from this perspective, everything will shift. No longer will you NEED the job, the man, the woman, the money, or the prize. You may desire it, but you know that acquiring it does not make or break your happiness. If you get your dream job, great. But if you don't get your dream job, that might be great too! With this, the world turns from threatening to safe, from unknown to known. No matter what happens, your safety and happiness are not threatened. You know you have everything you need, and so that is what shows up!

How did I make this shift in my life? I started here, with the power of choice.

CHOOSE AGAIN

A Course in Miracles emphasizes practicality over theology. It wants you to have experiences that prove to you what the course is saying. To help us do this, the course uses the principle of choice and choosing again, time after time.

You have the power to think about things differently. You have the power to think from love and not from fear. It is up to you to change your mind, and then you can watch the world change around you.

Only you can prove this to yourself.

I have faith in you, because you are me – and I, my friend, am you.

We are ALL ONE in spirit.

WHAT DOES *A COURSE IN MIRACLES* SAY ABOUT CHANGE?

You were given free will, but to think that God could or would want to change you goes against everything that He is.

God knows who you are. He knows you are eternal love. He knows you are safe and at home, but you do not know you are safe. The Holy Spirit was God's answer to your belief in the separation from Him. The Holy Spirit, the Voice for God, is in the One Mind, which we all share. So, it is literally up to you to take what you choose seriously.

- What do you want in your life?
- What do you believe?

The course says change is scary to our ego mind because the first change it experienced was separation. So, it now equates change with separation, and it remembers the sin, guilt, and fear that came with it. Unlike the Holy Spirit, which loves you and holds God's plan for you, the ego mind is unaware of what you truly are and is wholly mistrustful of everything it perceives. That is why change makes you, and most people, feel frightened.

We are often comfortable with where we are and frightened to change because, just like God, we love what we have made. We even love our mis-creations.

So, go gently with yourself. The ego mind does not give up its position easily. However, it has been my experience that if I take a small step each day over the course of many years, I can look back and see how far my thinking has come.

- I realize I am no longer hooked by old patterns.
- I see how the drama in my life has calmed.

And often, to my delight and surprise, I find moments of unplanned happiness and joy in even the littlest of things – like looking out at the fluffy silver clouds with their necklace of dark evergreens on a cold winter morning. I feel God within all things.

What thought system do you want to follow: a thought system that is uncompromising in its commitment to love and eternal life, or a thought system that is all tied up with sin, guilt, and fear?

We get to choose. That is the power of this very moment: you get to choose.

When we choose not to judge, not to criticize, not to see the fear, we move just a little farther away from the shadow and into the light. In these moments, the essence of who we truly are is realized more and more. It is a mighty adventure, and it is one that is well worth undertaking.

As we venture out into our new worlds, we realize that the things that come to "try us" are not meant to defeat us. Instead, they are meant to uplift us. I love how the course puts it in the following quote:

> "Trials are but lessons that you failed to learn, presented once again,
> so where you made a faulty choice before you now can make a better one,
> and thus escape all pain that what you chose before has brought to you.
> In every difficulty, all distress, and each perplexity
> Christ calls to you and gently says, 'My brother, choose again.'
> He would not leave one source of pain unhealed,
> nor any image left to veil the truth.
> He would not leave you comfortless,
> alone in dreams of hell,
> but would release your mind from everything
> that hides His face from you."
>
> T, 31, VIII, 3:1-5

CHOOSE ONE THOUGHT SYSTEM

"The way out of conflict between two opposing thought systems is clearly to choose one and relinquish the other."

T, 5, V, B, 5:1

CHOICE LIES IN CHOOSING TRUTH.

"There is a choice that you have power to make when you have seen the real alternatives. Until that point is reached you have no choice, and you can but decide how you would choose the better to deceive yourself again. This course attempts to teach no more than that the power of decision cannot lie in choosing different forms of what is still the same illusion and the same mistake. All choices in the world depend on this; you choose between your brother and yourself, and you will gain as much as he will lose, and what you lose is what is given him. How utterly opposed to truth is this, when all the lesson's purpose is to teach that what your brother loses you have lost, and what he gains is what is given you."

T, 31, IV, 8:1-5

THERE ARE NO IDLE THOUGHTS

"There are no idle thoughts. All thinking produces form at some level."

T, 2, VI, 9:13-14

THOUGHTS HAVE A STARTING POINT

"Every system of thought must have a starting point. It begins with either a making or a creating, a difference we have already discussed. Their resemblance lies in their power as foundations. Their difference lies in what rest upon them. Both are cornerstones for systems of belief by which one lives. It is a mistake to believe that a thought system based on lies is weak. Nothing made by a child of God is without power. It is essential to realize this, because otherwise you will be unable to escape from the prison you have made."

T, 3, VII, 1:1-7

THE THOUGHT GOD HOLDS OF YOU REMAINS PERFECTLY UNCHANGED

"Thoughts seem to come and go. Yet all this means is that you are sometimes aware of them, and sometimes not. An unremembered thought is born again to you when it returns to your awareness. Yet it did not die when you forgot it. It was always there, but you were unaware of it. The Thought God holds of you is perfectly unchanged by your forgetting. It will always be exactly as it was before the time when you forgot and will be just the same when you remember."

T, 30, III, 4:1-7

THOUGHTS INCREASE BY BEING GIVEN AWAY AND BELIEVED

"Thoughts increase by being given away. The more who believe in them the stronger they become. Everything is an idea. How, then, can giving and losing be associated?"

T, 5, I, 2:2-5

YOU LIVE AND TEACH THE THOUGHT SYSTEM YOU HAVE DEVELOPED

"Once you have developed a thought system of any kind, you live by it and teach it."

T, 6, Introduction, 2:4

PART FOUR

LET'S GET PRACTICAL:
Putting Reverse Thinking In To Day-To-Day Action

"No one has ever lived who has not experienced some light and some thing.
No one, therefore, is able to deny truth totally, even if he thinks he can."

T, 3, II, 1:7-8

INTRODUCTION

THE RECOGNITION THAT YOU DO NOT UNDERSTAND IS A PREREQUISITE!

"The recognition that you do not understand is a prerequisite for undoing your false ideas.
These exercises are concerned with practice, not with understanding.
You do not need to practice what you already understand.
It would indeed be circular to aim at understanding,
and assume that you have it already."

W, L9, 1:4-7

"It is difficult for the untrained mind to believe that what it seems to picture is not there.
This idea can be quite disturbing, and may meet with active resistance in any number of forms.
Yet that does not preclude applying it.
No more than that is required for these or any other exercises.
Each small step will clear a little of the darkness away, and understanding will finally come to lighten
every corner of the mind that has been cleared of the debris that darkens it."

W, L9, 2:1-5

THE EARTH IS A CLASSROOM

The earth is a classroom where we come to learn. Everything we do here is for our higher good, as it can be used as a tool to teach us about love or about separation and fear.

Ultimately, we decide what we are going to learn at what time. However, the curriculum is always the same for everyone.

You came here to forgive all the illusions you have made up about yourself and others. In reality, you came here to reclaim who you truly are: the light and love of God. But these are simply words that few can hear. In order for these words to mean anything, we need practical experiences. We need to prove it to ourselves.

HERE ARE SOME WAYS YOU CAN START

A. START SIMPLE: Reverse Your Thoughts.

Whenever you think something negative or find yourself feeling uncomfortable, make an effort to focus on what you are thinking. Just try to observe your thought, then turn this thought upside-down. This is the most simple and profound practice.

REVERSE THINKING

"Seek not to change the world.
Choose to change your mind about the world."
T, 21, Introduction, 1:7

If you think, *"I am poor,"*
turn it upside down: *"I am rich."*
Remember that you are rich in your spiritual heritage. You are everything that God is, because you are an extension of God. By looking at life from a spiritual perspective and not just a physical perspective, you can acknowledge God's truth about you and not just your own small opinions of yourself. Let's try another example.

If you think, *"I do not know anything,"*
turn it upside down: *"I do know everything."*
You know everything within your spirit. You are perfect and eternal, and you have access to the knowledge within just like everyone else. However, you cover this up within your mind when you believe you don't know. You then actually do not know, because you yourself are putting up a block to the knowledge. Trust yourself to receive what you already know.

Open up to "what is" within you.

B. STUDY WITH OTHERS: Set up an *A Course in Miracles* study group.

A Course in Miracles is a practical self-study guide. It says:

> *"This is a course in mind training.*
> *All learning involves attention and study at some level."*
> T, 1, VII, 4:1-2

If you are drawn to study more about *A Course in Miracles*, why not set up your own study group with some friends? You do not have to be the teacher; remember, everyone is both teacher and student. All you need is a sincere desire to learn how to improve your life. I am happy for you to use the study group format I have used for years.

DOWNLOAD MY STUDY GROUP FORMAT FROM MY WEBSITE
- Go to www.dianelundmiracles.ca
- Click on Free Downloads on the sidebar
- Click on Free Study Group Format

C. GET INSPIRED: Monday Miracle Moments

Sign up for our Free Monday Miracle Moments inspirational cards and join our closed Facebook Group to see a weekly video on the card.

People in my study groups love to pull cards with inspirational quotes from *A Course in Miracles*. It seems people always pull the card that addresses a question they have expressed or comments on the evening's reading.

Monday Miracle Moments are an electronic version of pulling an *A Course in Miracles* inspirational card. Trust that the universe will be delivering the message you need to your email each week on Monday morning. The card is laid out beautifully, (an example can be seen on the right) so it can be printed out and put up on your wall to inspire you throughout the week!

In addition, you can request to become a member of the closed Facebook page entitled "Diane Lund's Monday Miracles." There I will post a short video about the weekly inspirational message. I think of it as bite-sized learning, because you can dip your toe into *A Course in Miracles* wisdom without joining a group. To learn more, follow the links below.

SIGN UP FOR MONDAY MIRACLE MOMENTS
• www.bit.ly/mondaymiracles

TO WATCH THE VIDEOS
Become a member of our closed Monday Miracle
Moment Group
www.facebook.com/groups/dianelundmiracles/

**D. PRACTICE: Put Reverse Thinking to Work
In Your Life.**

There are three online courses based on Turn Your
World Upside Down to Get Your Life Right Side
Up: Book I entitled:
- Life's Big Questions,
- Relationships,
- Work and Career.

In addition, there are three more onlinecourses
based on Turn Your World Upside Down to Get
Your Life Right Side Up: Book II entitled:
- Health,
- Conflict and Fear, and
- Happiness.

"Miracles occur
naturally as
expressions
of love.

The real miracle
is the love that
inspires them.

T, 1, 3:1-2

Each course runs for six weeks online. For start dates go to **www.dianelundmiracles.com**
The format for each of the courses is as follows.
- **READ** the story.
- **DISCUSS** some quotes from *A Course in Miracles* which illustrate the spiritual principle we
  are studying.
- **EXERCISE** reverse thinking by reviewing the exercises for the week.
- **JOURNAL** about your experience over the week.
- **MEDITATE** to quiet the mind.

In my life, I have found it is always better doing things together. If we want to get to our true home, we
must embrace each other – all our brothers and sisters.

TRY ONE LESSON FOR FREE
- Go to dianelundmiracles.com
- Click on "Free Downloads" on the sidebar
- Click on "Free Demo Lesson"

E. SHARE YOUR MIRACLES ONLINE: Post on our open Facebook pages.
A Course in Miracles is a prove-it-to-yourself course. When you practice changing your mind and see remarkable transformations, it always feels good to share. Personally, I always find it inspiring and enlightening to read other people's miracles. I invite you to share your miracles on our Facebook pages.

- **www.facebook.com/dianelundmiracles/**
- **www.facebook.com/groups/dianelundmiracles/**

F. RESISTANCE: Do You Feel Resistance to Doing the Work?

> *"Change is always fearful to the separated because they cannot conceive of it as
> a move towards healing the separation. They always perceive it as a move
> toward further separation because the separation was their first experience of change.
> You believe that if you allow no change to enter into your ego you will find peace.
> This profound confusion is possible only if you maintain that the same thought system
> can stand on two foundations."*
>
> T, 4, I, 2:2-5

What does the above quote mean? It means that the very first separation we ever experienced was separation from God, and we experienced it as sinful, guilty, and worthy of punishment. So, using our past to determine our future, we projected that idea and now believe that all change will be like the first separation – painful and tough. However, it is also painful to continue doing the things that never work. The ego has hundreds of strategies that do not work to bring us peace.

Let's review some of the things that do not work.

60 Things That Do Not Help to Bring Peace

1. Trying to change others
2. Trying to cope and feeling drained
3. Leaving or avoiding your feelings
4. Explaining to people how they cause you misery
5. Overeating
6. Overdoing
7. Overworking
8. Overachieving
9. Crying and screaming
10. Negotiating
11. Lying to yourself
12. Lying to others
13. Getting out of it with drugs
14. Drinking too much
15. Blaming
16. Frustration
17. Yelling
18. Anger
19. Confusion
20. Getting another partner
21. Getting another job
22. Getting another car
23. Getting out of town
24. Pretending
25. Going blank
26. Hoarding
27. Not sharing
28. Hating
29. Stealing
30. Gossiping
31. Complaining
32. Criticizing
33. Lusting after things
34. Greed
35. Dis-ease
36. Cursing
37. Abandoning
38. Fighting
39. Freezing
40. Roleplaying
41. Striving
42. Doubting
43. Making up stories that hurt us
44. Feeding on stories that hurt
45. Putting on a brave face
46. Guilt
47. Punishment
48. Revenge
49. Suffering
50. Sacrificing
51. Tolerating
52. Depression
53. Drama
54. Chaos
55. Ignoring
56. Shrinking
57. Defences
58. Attack
59. Conflict
60. Wishing it would all just go away!

Everyone will have their own special list of things they have tried that do not work, and the ego wants you to find more. There are thousands of ways to separate you from yourself and from others, and none of them work. But you can try them all – there is no judgment. Remember, the course says:

> *"You can wait, delay, paralyze yourself,*
> *or reduce your creativity almost to nothing.*
> *But you cannot abolish it.*
> *You can destroy your medium of communication, but not your potential.*
> *You did not create yourself."*
>
> T, 1, V, 1:5-8

> *"The basic decision of the miracle-minded is not to wait on time any longer than is necessary.*
> *Time can waste as well as be wasted."*
>
> T, 1, V 2:1

PRACTICE IS NECESSARY.
Here are some simple things you can try that do work.

60 Things That Do Help to Bring Peace
1. Do not try to change others
2. Ask for help
3. Feel gratitude
4. Forgive someone
5. Forgive yourself instead of judging yourself
6. Listen deeply
7. Give grievances to God/Universe/Holy Spirit
8. Ask for peace in your life
9. Share
10. Join in
11. Give to yourself
12. Give to others
13. Be honest with yourself
14. Surrender
15. Extend love
16. Be gentle with yourself

17. Be gentle with others
18. Feel the love in your heart
19. Rest in God
20. Have faith
21. Treat everyone like you would want to be treated
22. Undo a judgment, or even two
23. Drop a long-held judgment about a person, place, or thing
24. Be willing to hear the small voice within
25. Feel inspired
26. Give up striving
27. Stop worrying
28. Acknowledge that you do not know
29. Trust your inner voice
30. Align with your right mind
31. Pray
32. Check in with yourself
33. Watch for synchronicities
34. Stop yelling
35. Stop arguing
36. Let go
37. Rest
38. Meditate
39. Laugh at yourself
40. Sing someone else's praises
41. Practice forgiveness
42. Hug someone
43. Compliment someone
44. Be generous
45. Be light-hearted
46. Stop telling old victim stories
47. Ask for a shift in perception
48. Start a miracle journal
49. Be a miracle worker
50. Stay calm
51. Open your heart
52. Accept what "is"
53. Open yourself to grace
54. Be abundant
55. Be true to yourself
56. Be patient
57. Be kind
58. Be open
59. Be heartfelt
60. Be

PRACTICE RELEASING JUDGMENTS OF YOURSELF AND OTHERS

A Course in Miracles states that I can only escape the world I see by giving up judgmental and attack thoughts. There is no point lamenting or trying to change the world; it is incapable of change because it is merely an effect of our thoughts. You cannot be saved from the world, but you can escape from its cause.

Practice Changing Your Mind.

The problem is never "out there," it is always "in here" – in our mind's way of thinking. The mind is the cause while the world is the effect of the one mind that we all share. So, to change your mind, try following these simple steps:

1. Identify the thought.
2. Let it go to the Holy Spirit and ask for help in seeing things another way.
3. Flip the thought on its head.
4. Replace a thought based in fear with a thought based in love.

For Example:

Identify the thought that hurts: *My partner never listens to me.*

Give this thought to the Holy Spirit: *Take this thought, I will not judge it.*

Flip the thought: *I never listen to myself.*

Replace with a 180-degree thought that works: *I will listen to my inner voice.*

> *"The way out of two opposing thought systems is clearly to choose one and relinquish the other."*
>
> T, 6, B, 5:1

G. COLLABORATIVE MIRACLES BOOKS: Write your miracle story and become an author with me.

A miracle, according to *A Course in Miracles*, is a change in perception from thinking from fear to thinking from love. We will be creating a series of books where people collaborate to share their miracle stories.

If you have a story you would like to share in one of these upcoming books, please go the website to see how you can apply to take part.
www.dianelundmiracles/books/collaborative

REMEMBER, WE HAVE A MISSION HERE.

"We have a mission here.
We did not come to reinforce the madness
that we once believed in.
Let us not forget the goal that we accepted.
It is more than just our happiness alone we came to gain.
What we accept as what we are
proclaims what everyone must be,
along with us.
Fail not your brothers,
or you fail yourself.
Look lovingly on them,
that they may know
that they are part of you
and you of them."

W, L139, 9:1-7

CONNECT WITH OUR COMMUNITY
Join Reverend Diane C. Lund and her community of like-minded spiritual students online to engage further with the material presented in this book.

BOOK
Turn Your World UPSIDE DOWN to Get Your Life RIGHT SIDE UP!
Reverse Thinking based on *A Course in Miracles*.
Book I: Life's Big Questions, Relationships, Work and Career.
Purchase on Amazon or on my website
- www.dianelundmiracles.com

VISIT THE WEBSITE
The website is designed to be an online lighthouse and supportive community that guides, inspires, and awakens your spirit.
- www.dianelundmiracles.com

LIKE OUR FACEBOOK PAGES
- www.facebook.com/dianelundmiracles
- www.facebook.com/groups/dianelundmiracles/

FREE ELECTRONIC MONDAY MIRACLE MOMENT CARDS
Receive weekly downloadable cards with an inspirational quote from *A Course in Miracles* every Monday by email. Sign up at:
- bit.ly/mondaymiracles

WATCH MONDAY MIRACLE MOMENT VIDEOS
Join our closed Facebook group to view short videos about each of the Monday Miracle Moment cards.
- www.facebook.com/groups/dianelundmiracles

ORDER MONDAY MIRACLE MOMENT CARD DECKS
The Monday Miracle Moment cards come in eight different coloured decks: rose, tangerine, marigold, aqua, jade, violet, orchid, and crimson. Order online.
- www.dianelundmiracles.com/shop

LEARN MORE ABOUT REVEREND DIANE C. LUND

CREATIVE PORTFOLIO
- www.creativewonders.ca

FACEBOOK
- www.facebook.com/creativewondersinc

LINKED-IN
- www.linkedin.com/in/dianelund/

PINTEREST
- www.pinterest.ca/seeourwonders/

E-BOOK
Ready Aim Fire: They Keys To Unlocking Business Creativity
- www.bit.ly/readyaimfirePDF

AWARDS
- **2019 International Silver Award** – Most Original Calendar World Calendar Awards - Multifaith Calendar 2019: Coming Together: Exploring New Connections
- **2017 International Silver Summit Award** - Online Marketing Effectiveness for Vancouver's North Shore Tourism campaign
- **2017 The Visioneers International Network** - Lifetime Achievement Award for Innovation and Entrepreneurship
- **2017 International Bronze Summit Creative Award** - Print Speciality
- **2017 International Judges Finalist Summit Creative Award** - Print
- **Chamber of Commerce Business Excellence Award for Best Busines**s - Creative Wonders Communications
- **Ethics in Actions Award** - Community Care. For "exceeding the vast majority of the CBSR (Canadian Business for Social Responsibility) guidelines, and showing huge heart by giving an unheard of 50% of profits or 15% of revenues to their community in support of building a better world." – N. Bradshaw Founder CBSR